Robert Spindler

Recent Westerns

Robert Spindler

Recent Westerns

Deconstruction and Nostalgia in Contemporary Western Film

Tectum Verlag

Robert Spindler

Recent Westerns.
Deconstruction and Nostalgia in Contemporary Western Film
ISBN: 978-3-8288-9744-1
Umschlagabbildung: Robert Spindler

Besuchen Sie uns im Internet
www.tectum-verlag.de

Bibliografische Informationen der Deutschen Nationalbibliothek
Die Deutsche Nationalbibliothek verzeichnet diese Publikation in der Deutschen Nationalbibliografie; detaillierte bibliografische Angaben sind im Internet über http://dnb.ddb.de abrufbar.

To Konrad Spindler

Acknowledgments

I would like to thank Sonja Bahn for supplying secondary literature, films, and inspiration. Bert Walser has helped by suggesting and providing films and literature, by giving ideas, and by a common interest in film. Hilde Wolfmeyer provided a great part of the films and counsel on journals and reviews. I was introduced to many of the Westerns discussed here by Stephan Colvin, who inspired this paper by a shared interest in the genre. Helpful advice was given by Susanne Pichler, Mario Klarer, and Gudrun Grabher. Martin Weidinger's friendly correspondence proved very valuable. Crucial guidance and motivation was given by Dorothee Spindler.

Grateful thanks are due to Arno Heller for the unproblematic collaboration. His geniality, personal involvement and interest in the subject, and sincere devotion to scholarship and his fields of study have been appreciated.

Table of Contents

1. Introduction

When I walked out of the cinema after seeing *3:10 to Yuma* (2007), I had the feeling that for one instant I could imagine what it must have been like for audiences at the heyday of the Hollywood Western to leave the theater after experiencing a state-of-the-art blockbuster of the genre. Significantly a remake of one great classic of 1956, the 2007 *3:10 to Yuma* sports everything a modern audience could wish for: popular stars, lavish production value, spectacular action sequences, and picturesque cinematography are supposed to make the film an entertaining and visually impressive experience, even for today's special-effect-spoiled viewers. And while certain elements are taken from the original almost one-to-one and still seem to work (like great parts of the dialogue), significant changes have been made in the film's ending, for example, apparently to adapt to a present-day audience that demands less straightforward solutions to more complicated problems. On the other hand, leaving the cinema after *The Assassination of Jesse James by the Coward Robert Ford* (2007) was a wholly different experience. Certainly this is a film according to modern viewers' tastes as well, and thus shares some features with *3:10 to Yuma* (2007). However, it leaves only a secondary role to the elements of entertainment, and suggests that to some problems there is no solution at all: the search for the man behind the Jesse James myth might be one such.

A thing that both films have in common, though, is that they are undeniably Westerns. The announcement of these two films along with the production and release of a number of other true and not so true Westerns in the last few years was the main motivation and inspiration to write about the genre's present state in this paper. But the hope that the release of these films was to be the indication of the final revival of the Hollywood Western might prove a bit too optimistic. Any wishful thinking in that direction is regularly dismissed in literature, a tradition kept up by experts on the field since at least the seventies. In 1974 Pauline Kael pronounced the Western genre dead, while "a few more Westerns may still struggle in" (qtd. in Lenihan 148). Hanisch reads *Heaven's Gate* (1980) as the "last Western" and strongly undermines and ridicules any notions of a Western Renaissance that might be triggered by the release of two or three new films per year (408). The most up-to-date instance of this view is Weidinger, who sees no chance of a true revival in spite of the release of *Open Range* (2003) and *The Missing* (2003) (*Nationale Mythen* 249). So, although some considerably popular and artistically innovative Westerns have been released since the publication of Weidinger's account, this paper shall refrain from proclaiming a resurrection of the genre or making any future predictions in that direction. But at the same time, the death of the Western shall also not be accepted as easily. Instead, a synchronic view will be applied: as long as films are being made that define themselves as Westerns, however little their number in relation to past decades, a Western genre must inevitably exist. Hence, for the purposes of this paper, major film productions since roughly the year 2000 will be regarded as the representation of the genre at present, as the recent Western and the shape it takes.

This is best done by tracing common tendencies in the newest examples that set them apart from former "eras" of Western film history. It appears that these "eras" are favorably made to correlate with subsequent decades.[1] So the task will be to evaluate what characterizes the Westerns produced since the year 2000 as opposed to, for example, those of the 1960s or 1980s. Not an easy task when looking at the fact that there is hardly anything the Western has not yet seen in its more than 100 years in the saddle. Most people know that the Western at one point gained complexity, lost popularity, began to deconstruct its own myth, and is now generally considered dead. But that this did not just happen very recently and in one straight line, the average movie-goer is often unaware of.

This paper examines how the most recent Western films tend to take up, revive and romanticize traditional Wild West mythology on the one hand, while further deconstructing these myths on the other hand. A general chapter on the Western genre will first focus on the problem of the relation between historical facts and Wild West fiction (related to the aspects of deconstruction and mythology), provide a short history of the Western film, and introduce the most prominent representatives of the latest years. In the main part, four relevant example films will be analyzed in detail. Aspects of predominant ideologies, gender, ethnicity, morality, mythology, and historicity will be considered to investigate how the recent Western can be categorized, where its position is in relation to the traditional formula Western, and how it reflects on the present sociopolitical and cultural context. On this foundation, this paper aims to demonstrate the opposition and unification of nostalgia and deconstruction in recent Wild West cinema, and will try to describe the particularities of the Western of the present time in a concluding chapter.

2. The Western Genre: from the Beginnings to the Present

This chapter will provide the necessary background information for a treatment of recent Wild West cinema. The Western genre itself will be introduced by a comment on the problem of historicity in Western fiction and film, and an indispensable overview of the history of the Western, as characteristic features of representatives of the genre changed significantly according to each generation. As this paper also focuses on the Western of a specific generation, a rough categorization of Westerns by "eras" will be approached, with special regard to the aspects of the deconstruction of myths and Western nostalgia at each epoch.

The dimensions that the Western genre and its mythology have taken on in the course of just more than a century are all the more impressive when seen in relation to the actual historical period they claim to represent. When disregarding earlier frontier themes, like, for example, the Indian Wars which served as the background for James F. Cooper's writings (whom many see as the founding father of frontier literature (e.g. Snodgrass 78-9; Brown 421)), strictly speaking the actual period of the Wild West is seen as covering not more than 30 years (*Spiel mir das Lied*). The frontier, the open range, and with them, cowboy- and rustler-romanticism are generally agreed upon to have ended during the early 1890s (cf. Hanisch 12; Heller, *Amerikanischer Südwesten* 168). The term "Western" is often used synonymously with Western film, but a whole universe of literature, dime novels, circus-shows, art, and country music in and outside of America are not to be ignored. While some of these branches have apparently already seen their height in popularity, like circus-shows, and, admittedly, the film, others, like the country music and dime novel industries, are still huge (Hanisch 408; Weidinger, *Nationale Mythen* 248). To try to explain this much-discussed phenomenon of the fascination for the West in popular culture would go beyond the scope and immediate relevancy of this paper. It shall only be suggested that the force of attraction of the Wild West seems to be twofold: next to escapism and the romantic longing for a simple, rural life close to nature and past virtues and ideals stands the deterrence of everyday life-threatening violence and adventure. Fenin and Everson see the relevancy of the Western genre in its role as a warning "against a return to frontier violence--although it still provides 'the vehicle for our dreams.'"

Unfortunately, all of the branches of the genre listed above were and still are represented to the greatest part by pulp fiction and kitsch, and to a large extent this also applies to the Western film. However, film-historically, culturally, and artistically relevant Westerns are abundant. Peculiarly, the share of such films produced at a certain time tends to be inversely proportional to the general popularity of the genre (one may take, for example, the more sophisticated films of the 1970s, when the genre had lost much of its popularity). This seems to be good news for our time, as Westerns made up only a minute proportion of annual Hollywood productions in recent years. With the endeavor to create artistically relevant films comes a greater awareness and pursuit of historically authentic portrayals of the frontier, and as production value standards and audience expectations rise, this is especially true of the recent Western. Hence, the aspect of historicity in the Western genre deserves special attention here.

2.1. Fact and Fiction

Distortions of reality for the sake of myth-creation could be witnessed in the Western genre practically from the moment it was born and while frontier history was still being written. Before the invention of film, painters, authors, and even photographers did their best to provide especially Eastern audiences with portrayals of the West that satisfied their romanticized ideas of the lives of settlers, Native Americans, and Western heroes--historical figures such as Wyatt Earp, Wild Bill Hickock, or Buffalo Bill (the latter three would in the course of time all get a chance to do so themselves in Wild-West-shows and stage performances). Indeed, fact and fiction were entwined to such a degree that their separation still causes a problem for historians today (Leonardy 106). Paintings distributed in the East would idealize agrarian living conditions far from the truth of makeshift dugout homes and claim shanties (Bogue 298). Later works of famous artists such as Charles M. Russell or Frederic Remington would depict the cowboy profession in a nostalgic, romantic, and stylized way (Dippie 693), or exaggerate frontier violence much beyond its actual dimensions (Brown 393) (Fig. 1). The greater the temporal distance between actual events and their fictionalized accounts, the more the legends thrived and got split off from historical facts (Hanisch 12). Dippie claims that the "combination of fiction, showmanship, and art that planted the cowboy's image in the public's mind came at a time when nostalgia was already cloaking the West in the romance of faded youth and better yesterdays" and concludes that Western art is not about historical realities, but cultural assumptions (695). That the same is true for the Western film, probably nobody will deny. Still, since the earliest days of Wild West cinema, the industry has made new claims for historical accuracy in their films. Hanisch points out that especially in the 1950s films tried to trump each other in realism (7). However, major problems have remained. In the following, a selective choice of themes in the Western will be looked at in trying to answer the question of how far from the truth Western films actually are.

Fig. 1. *What an Unbranded Cow Has Cost.* Frederic Remington (1861-1909). Oil on canvas, 1895 (from Milner, O'Connor, and Sandweiss 392).

Frontier violence

Disregarding the Indian wars for the moment, this section will focus on only two aspects of frontier violence, the feuds of cattle barons versus small-time ranchers, and typified shootouts between gunmen. The exhaustive violence depicted in Westerns is obviously not a mere vile product of the imagination of screenwriters and directors, as undisputed historical accounts of numerous vigilante wars, gunfights, and instances of lynching show. Brown offers a theory to explain these phenomena, namely a number of beliefs and ideologies that programmed Westerners to commit violence (393). The "doctrine of no duty to retreat," for example, an alteration from common English law, said that the American has the right to stand one's ground for self-defense in a confrontation which threatens to become violent, as opposed to the obligation to flee, if possible, in English law. Similarly, the "imperative of personal self-redress" tempted into the use of violence as an ideology to settle disputes by personal initiative. Another closely related example of these beliefs is the "ideology of vigilantism." Vigilantism was thus justified by the rights for self-preservation ("the first law of nature"), revolution (justifying vigilantism in analogy to the revolution against Britain in 1776, for example), and popular sovereignty (seeing the people as above a law which seemed ineffective in the face of frontier crime) (Brown 395-6). Although there is no room to go into detail here, it shall be indicated that remnants of these aspects still shape American society and culture strongly today, and a possible influence on contemporary film must not be dismissed.

Taking for granted that the beliefs and ideologies mentioned above and other, similar ones, characterized the predominant system of values among the white population of the American West during the frontier era, some of the violent events that serve as the subject matter for Western films gain credibility, and their depictions, as a consequence, authenticity. In fact, the extent of violence of the period has been estimated equivalent to a civil war and termed the "Western Civil War of Incorporation" (Brown 396). Disputes over landed property, grazing rights, money, political power, and of "who came first," and consequently tensions between cattle kings, cowboys, small ranchers, farmers, and rustlers in the open range marked the period between 1870 and 1890, with the less powerful parties desperately trying to resist the land-monopolizing thrust of big cattlemen (Heller, *Amerikanischer Südwesten* 158; Brown 401). The Lincoln Country War is one climactic example for such a feud. Incorporating businessmen, financial issues, and alleged insurance fraud, it escalated in the rally of a vigilante army of 40 men, killings, shootouts, and a five-day gun battle, which only few (among them Billy the Kid) survived (Heller, *Amerikanischer Südwesten* 161). In contrast to the Lincoln County War stands the Johnson County War. No less famous, also because it employed a large group of vigilantes, the "Regulators," it ended in a finale without bloodshed, in which the vigilante group had to be saved from a posse of citizens by the U.S. cavalry. Michael Cimino used this historical event as the background to his epic *Heaven's Gate* (1980). Despite being the greatest financial failure in the history of the Western film, it is now generally considered artistically valuable (cf. Hembus, *Lexikon* 298-300; Weidinger, *Nationale Mythen* 150). But as a reproduction of the Johnson County War it remains inaccurate, as it depicts the finale as a fierce shootout on a battleground which leaves hardly any survivors to witness the oncoming cavalry.

Many of the notorious Western shootouts and duels which served as an inspiration for a disproportionally large number of Western films were ultimately part of the Western Civil War of Incorporation. But how did shootouts and duels take place in reality, compared to their fictional portrayals in Westerns? The stereotypical duel which decides over life and death of opponents by how fast they are on the draw is beginning to be accepted as a myth by the general public now. In the documentary *Spiel mir das Lied vom Western*, a present-day showman, the supposed "fastest man on the draw alive," admits that there is not one recorded incident in actual history of a duel decided by the faster draw. Scenes as in *A Gunfight* (1970), which has Johnny Cash practicing the speed of his draw in anticipation of a duel with Kirk Douglas, or most characteristically Sergio Leone's "Dollar trilogy," in which the duel is celebrated in overlong, suspense-building scenes, with "technical effects [...] deliberately overstated" (Frayling, *Spaghetti Westerns* 180), may be regarded as mere fiction.

However, it seems that duels in themselves were no scarcity. Among other examples, Brown mentions U.S. president Andrew Jackson to have killed a man in a duel as a frontier man before his political career, and a David S. Terry to have done the same before being shot himself in a man-to-man confrontation (394, 401). The procedure of these "duels," whether man to man, based on rules, carried out with an emphasis on fairness, etc., is not mentioned here. But Brown does in fact point out the "Code of the West" as a code of honor, almost reminiscent of medieval, knightly virtues (395). Although the concept appears rather idealized, it seems that a gunfight carried out under certain prescriptive conditions could occur legitimately (Brown 395). The procedure of one such duel which is assumed to be historically well-founded is the killing of Dave Tutt by James Butler "Wild Bill" Hickock in what became the "prototypical western showdown" (Brown 401). Supposedly it served as a model for a similar scene in the influential Western novel *The Virginian* by Owen Wister, and was consequently fixed in the American mind as the "central formulaic event in the Western fiction of print and film" (Brown 419). However, besides being only one overly distributed instant, this event is described as a "walkdown," which does indicate a face-to-face confrontation between two men, but neither any long waiting periods of anticipation, nor any emphasis on a faster draw.

On the other hand, shootouts between groups of men, or a single man facing a group must have occurred at least equally often, and their depictions in Westerns can be viewed as closer to reality than most duel scenes. The legendary gunfight at the O.K. Corral, involving such big names as Wyatt Earp, Doc Holliday, and the Clanton Gang is only the most well-known instant. A less well-known Walter J. Crow is said to have killed five settlers in a single shootout on his own, setting a record that none of the most prominent Western gunmen could break in their lifetime (Brown 400). So, next to a truckload of films dealing with historical events like the gunfight at the O.K. Corral, purely fictional shootouts in such films as *High Noon* (1952), for example, seem to paint a more authentic picture of the West, at least in contrast to stereotypical "duel films."

Historical figures

The flamboyant historical figures of the West are what shaped its mythology most and contributed significantly to the enduring popularity of the genre and its many reinterpretations. Lawmen like Isaac J. Parker and Roy Bean, amazons like Calamity Jane and Belle Starr, conservative sheriffs and gunmen like Wyatt Earp and Wild Bill Hickock, or dissident social bandits like Billy the Kid and Jesse James have become legends inseparable from the Wild West universe. Especially gunmen like the latter four have enjoyed great appeal in Western fiction up until most recent times. The gulf between their real lives and the legends built on them has been the issue of much debate and shall shortly be introduced here.

How rapidly the biographies of some Western legends have often been twisted around and adapted to popular sensationalist demands is remarkable. In 1880, four years after Wild Bill Hickock's death, the first biography appeared in print, "eine in phantasievoller Sensationslust schwelgende Ansammlung sämtlicher Lügenmärchen, die über Hickock je verbreitet wurden" (Hembus, *Geschichte* 523). In the next year, Hickock was to be the main figure of interest in James William Buel's *Heroes of the Plains*, appreciated by a large readership as a reliable source for the chronicles of famous Westerners, but in reality only as authentic as a dime novel (Hembus, *Geschichte* 541). The first biography of Billy the Kid, written by his very killer Pat Garret (as grotesquely declared on the cover), is considered "widely inaccurate" (Brown 406). Especially remarkable in the instance of Billy the Kid is the transformation of his fictional character from a demonic criminal to a tragic-romantic hero, once the closer circumstances of his life became known--which does not mean that such accounts were less distorted and overdrawn (Heller, *Amerikanischer Südwesten* 164). Billy the Kid would eventually be depicted as a misguided juvenile, then as a sort of Robin Hood of the Southwest (Heller,

Amerikanischer Südwesten 165). Meanwhile, the real Billy the Kid was of historical insignificance (Heller, *Amerikanischer Südwesten* 162).

This tradition was then continued in film. Heller lists five generations of Billy the Kid films with great variety in the characterization of the ruinous youth, most of which reflect rather the sociopolitical circumstances of the time when they were made, instead of a historically faithful account of events (*Amerikanischer Südwesten* 165-7). Although Wild Bill Hickock has been less of a prominent hero, films involving his character and also beyond any historical foundation can be found throughout. One filmic interpretation of Wild Bill Hickock deserves special mentioning, though, which is the very recent television Western series *Deadwood* (2004-6). Featuring a *potpourri* of historical and fictional figures, it dramatizes episodes filled with historical detail around the actual town of Deadwood during the 1870s. Wild Bill Hickock is part of the first few episodes with constant allusions to his actual life and stay in Deadwood, before he finds his death in a sequence which obviously relies on recorded facts surrounding the killing of the historical figure of Hickock in 1876 (cf. Hembus, *Geschichte* 483-6). However, the series has other shortcomings, and will be mentioned again below. The case of Jesse James will be of greater relevance here and also receive a closer look later, in the discussion of *The Assassination of Jesse James by the Coward Robert Ford* (2007). For the moment, it shall only be suggested that the fictionalization of Jesse James' life took a course not unequal to that of Billy the Kid. Just two examples of classic Jesse James films, which depict the idealized outlaw according to trends and audience wants of their time, are *Jesse James* (1939) and its remake of 1957, *The True Story of Jesse James*. In *Jesse James*, which began the actual "new vogue for romanticizing the West's real outlaws" (Parkinson and Jeavons 46), the title character takes on the appearance of a farmer's boy hero in accordance with the depression era of the thirties, while *The True Story* depicts James as a fifties-teenager in remembrance of James Dean or Marlon Brando (Lenihan 142-3). In some respect, the title supplement "The True Story" in the latter probably only continues the tradition of absurd claims for historical authenticity.

To a curious modern viewer of Jesse James or Billy the Kid films, the question may arise how a sympathizing portrayal of personae who where actually criminals could evolve at all (leaving the somewhat naive Robin Hood myth of "taking from the rich and giving to the poor" aside: numerous bank and train robberies inevitably took a toll on peaceable farmers, ranchers, and townspeople (cf. Brown 399)). There is evidence that such outlaws enjoyed the favor and support of their society already during their lifetime. Brown divides the most prominent gunmen of the West into two groups: the "conservative winning side of the Western Civil War of Incorporation," like Wild Bill Hickock or Wyatt Earp (or the fictional "Virginian" of Wister's novel, see above) in opposition to the anti-incorporating side, generating a dissident social bandit myth from figures like Jesse James, Billy the Kid, or Gregorio Cortez (421). These "social bandits," lawbreakers paradoxically supported by a law-abiding society, were admired for their bravery and daring, and approved of for their expression of "discontents and grievances of those who would never dare commit such crimes on their own" (Brown 399). Contemporary photographs of Jesse James, posing with his gun drawn, record the ironical acknowledgment of his own popular bandit status (Brown 398) (Fig. 2). That the opposing side of Hickock or Earp would gain no less popularity and appeal, is explained by the highly ambivalent appeal of established power versus dissident protest among Americans (Brown 421). The successful application of outlaw figures of the West to interpret social phenomena of later decades, like rebellious teenagers in *The True Story of Jesse James*, or a self-destructive, nihilistic youth culture in *Young Guns* (1988) (another account of the Billy the Kid myth, cf. Heller, *Amerikanischer Südwesten* 167), underscores these theories. At the same time, though, it suggests the general historical inaccuracy of such Westerns.

Fig. 2. *Jesse James on Horseback.* Unidentified photographer. Tintype, c. 1870 (from Milner, O'Connor, and Sandweiss 398).

Native Americans

That the Western genre has done much to paint a picture of America's indigenous people which is inauthentic in a historical sense, and even dangerous in a sociocultural sense, is no secret nowadays. Even in the earliest days of cinema, a lack of respect for indigenous cultures complemented the necessity to satisfy audiences with a need for the exotic. Thomas A. Edison's kinetoscope shorts already included one dramatized "Hopi Snake Dance" in 1893 (Jojola 12). That early instances of stereotyping are not be regarded as insignificant is indicated by the fact that Native American protest against inaccurate and harmful depictions of their cultural history is not much younger than the history of narrative cinema itself: Champagne records a protest by Chippewa against the movie industry's distortions of Native Americans already in 1911 (268). Hanisch reads the treatment of Native Americans in film as a two-pole continuation of a white literary tradition: next to racist Indian imagery he places the sympathizing acknowledgment of the high culture of Native Americans and their status as the rightful owners of American soil (8). But only since the fifties Hanisch detects noteworthy attempts at faithful portrayals of Native Americans in film (8).

However, it still was (and is?) a long way to go until the problem of an appropriate depiction of the Native American could even be fully grasped by white filmmakers. The contributors to *Hollywood's Indian*, edited by Rollins and O'Connor, agree that Hollywood stereotypes have little to do with reality, but are divided in their opinions on newer, ambitious pro-Indian films, like the prototypical *Dances With Wolves* (1990): one party welcomes them, while the other is still distressed by them for various reasons. Among many others, one topical point of debate (though not applying to *Dances With Wolves* in this instance) is the employment of white actors to portray Native Americans. This has been much discussed in the pursuit of an answer to why a correlation between cast and role has been so hard to achieve (cf. Jojola). Even in the aftermath of *Dances With Wolves*, a new wave of Indian sympathy films featured examples of white actors playing the Native American lead, like *Thunderheart* (1992) or *Last of the Mohicans* (1992) (Jojola 15-6, 18). The only filmic representation of Indians that Jojola explicitly praises is the character of Old Lodge Skins, played by Chief Dan George in *Little Big Man* (1970) (13) (Fig. 3). This shows, however,--as the latter film is in itself a rather cynical comment on the fusion of fact and fiction--that a praiseworthy portrayal of Native Americans in whichever film is not synonymous with a historically authentic depiction, and further complicates the problem. Another phenomenon which Jojola points out, and which contributed to the complexity of the issue by distorting the viewpoint of white filmmakers, is that Native Americans began to act and behave like their stereotyped movie counterparts (at least until the establishment of the American Indian Movement in the late sixties) (13).[2]

Fig. 3. Chief Dan George as Chief Old Lodge Skins in *Little Big Man*. Still (from Rollins and O'Connor 123).

As Hollywood continued the creation and cultivation of myths even throughout the nineties, the then thriving ambition to present fairer pictures of Native Americans in film nevertheless has to be appreciated. In spite of remaining difficulties, the employment of Native American consultants, playwrights, and cultural experts in order to achieve more tribal precision, to feature real native languages, and hence to create more historically authentic depictions, was a revolutionary step in the development in American cinema (Jojola 18). How the treatment of these problems developed in recent years will be looked at below.

Women

Another shortcoming of the genre is then brought into play, namely its primary male orientation. Dippie points out that female presence in the male escapist fantasy of Western art is minimal, and the rare cases depict women in a limited number of set roles: "sunbonneted pioneer mothers, golden-hearted prostitutes, the occasional female outlaw" (695). The same applies to most Western films, which are almost exclusively told from a male perspective. Traditional Westerns can not offer more than stereotypical, simplistic versions of the lives of frontier women and female roles are made to fit the romantic vision of the West as understood by men (Butler 776). The few exceptions only seem to confirm the rules. Butler dismisses notorious female Western heroes like Calamity Jane, Belle Starr, or Annie Oakley as quirky exceptions "that affirmed the maleness of western society" (776). Even until very recently, films such as *The Quick and the Dead* (1995), which features a gun-slinging female hero, simply reverse the female role into a male one and arguably deviate from a historically faithful depiction even more so (cf. Weidinger, *Nationale Mythen* 151,153). Hence, the major problem in the characterization of women in the Western, similarly as that of Native Americans, seems to lie in the predominant white male viewpoint in the overwhelming majority of representations of the genre. However, I shall return to the issue of femininity in Westerns in the discussion of contemporary Westerns.

This paragraph has mainly presented a critical view of the historical inaccuracy in the Western genre, and nowadays most scholars will agree that the classic Western presents a distortion of reality. However, does this fact automatically oblige one to condemn the genre? Even devoted fans of Westerns seem to be aware that they are merely presented with romanticized myths. Consequential films preoccupied with the deconstruction of these myths do not necessarily present a historically more authentic account, but might simply turn certain stereotypes around to represent the other extreme of the scale. But there appears to be a certain ideology to defend the mythology as the very essence of the Western. Hanisch draws a parallel between the Western and fairy tales and defends the related naivety and straightforwardness of both (7). In *Spiel mir das Lied vom Western*, the popularity of the Western among the broad public is exposed as a faith in the poetic truth of events, next to an awareness of their fictionalization. And Hembus vehemently condemns the ambitions of newer films and literature to unmask and shatter myths in the pursuit of the historical truth (*Geschichte*, 8). But these approaches must be regarded as rather short-sighted when considering the depiction of female roles, Native Americans, or violent frontier ideologies in the Western. Not at last, as McCrisken and Pepper argue, because Hollywood plays a fundamental role in shaping the ideological content of American public history (64), stereotypical and historically inaccurate accounts of frontier life must be considered potentially harmful. Hence, a critical stance towards an overtly distorted reality in certain aspects of the Western must be maintained.

2.2. A Short History of the Western

This paragraph will provide a very basic history of the Western film in three sections. First, a chronological view will mark off significant eras in the genre's history. Then, for the particular relevance to later discussion, developments in the depiction of the Western hero throughout these eras will be traced, and at last some landmark films in the treatment of Native Americans will shortly be introduced. Of course the short essay presented here can by no means claim to be exhaustive and go into detail with the political and social backgrounds which shaped the Western throughout the twentieth century. Instead, only a selective choice of films, directors, or actors relevant to the contents of this paper is presented. Other films throughout American Western cinema history with less general recognition, but essential to following discussions which have not yet been mentioned and are not listed here will be brought up in the appropriate place later.

Eras in Western film history

The Great Train Robbery (1903) is considered the first American film to be taken seriously, and, typically enough, it is also the first Western (Hanisch 18). Depicting events based on real incidents not too distant in time,[3] it set off a true Western boom in the gradually developing film industry (Hanisch 23). Whole production companies depended entirely on these films in the following years, hundreds of cheaply made features of ten to twenty minutes length, which already covered the basic scope of Western themes: cowboy life, pioneers, stagecoach robberies, Indian wars, and historical figures and events (Hanisch 25-6).

Following a decline in popularity towards the late twenties, the thirties marked the beginning of a process in which the Western would get more and more complicated and structured in the course of three decades (Seeßlen and Weil 71). Seeßlen and Weil see the trigger for this in *The Virginian* (1929), a partially successful film based on Owen Wister's novel (see above) and starring Gary Cooper, as it allowed for the inner conflicts, motives, and principles of the protagonist to be scrutinized (69, 71). The year 1939 then saw a significant turn in the history of what began to look like a fading genre. Parkinson and Jeavons take the end of the depression and the impending war in Europe as an explanation for the readiness of Americans to take pride in the national progress of the frontier era again, and for the release of a whole string of innovative and influential films in this single year, which revolutionized and resurrected the genre (38). First and foremost *Stagecoach*, the beginning of a prolific collaboration of John Ford and John Wayne, with its mythic-poetic interpretation of the development of American society from the individual and the community, its symbolist depiction of the relationship between landscape and humans, and the dramatic standards it sets, is considered one of the most influential Westerns of all time (Seeßlen and Weil 78-80). So if any specific time in the history of American film deserves to be termed the classical period of the Western, is must be the years from 1939 to 1949, for, although the films of the fifties are justly much better known and appreciated as classics, they were already enriched by a new level of critical self-reflectiveness, and political and social commentary. Still, their thematic alterations according to the changing intellectual and political climate, their more critical assessment of ideals, and their comments on the social situation in the US, made the films of the fifties the most interesting and film-historically relevant Westerns until then (Lenihan 148; Hanisch 9). *Johnny Guitar* (1953) is just the most famous Western of the fifties which initiated alternative perspectives on women in the genre, though mostly through strong, but misguided female characters, who adopt typically male features, like lust for power and pugnacity (Seeßlen and Weil 132-4).

The genre had reached a zenith in popularity in the fifties, which it could never regain, and the annual release of films declined in numbers ever since then (Lenihan 148). Weidinger sees the genre's sexism particularly responsible for this (*Nationale Mythen* 246), while Seeßlen and Weil look for an explanation in the completion of the process of demystification which had taken its course (161). The motivations for the majority of producers to continue making Westerns now lay in such efforts as to shoot the "last Western," to pretend nothing had happened, or to create another large-scale epic Western in the spirit of tradition (Seeßlen and Weil 161). But most significant to the Western of the sixties and early seventies were the films of Sam Peckinpah, who ushered in the "Passion of the Western." As the most important Western director of this period, he presented a dismal image of the sad, bitter end of the Old West, in which its heroes, moral, rules, and confident vision of futurity are questioned (Weidinger, *Nationale Mythen* 148; Hanisch 384-5; Seeßlen and Weil 193). Peckinpah's most forceful Western is the shattering *The Wild Bunch* (1969), a visually stunning ode to violence plainly spelling out the death of the West, a portrait of exhausted heroism, and a blow to any comfortable vision of the legendary West (Parkinson and Jeavons 86-9). A film reluctant to any categorization, but nevertheless characteristic of the beginning seventies, is Robert Altman's *McCabe & Mrs. Miller* (1970), whose picturesque soundtrack and authentic visualization contrasts with its disenchanting depiction of an impotent anti-hero, the blatant reality of prostitution, and historical detail of the inevitable progress, which announces the end of the West. Arthur notes that Altman's desire to disturb viewers' expectations of what constitutes a "proper" Western is apparent in the presentation of a familiar lineup of elements from unfamiliar angles, "stripped of its romanticized, dualistic luster" (19).

In spite of the relatively meager output in American Westerns during the eighties and nineties, the films of these decades deserve due attention here, as especially the most recent developments in the genre might be of relevancy to this paper. Following the weak late seventies, the eighties clearly marked the greatest commercial and artistic low of the genre until then, and although Westerns kept being produced, they were no longer the success-guaranteed base of US cinema (Weidinger, *Nationale Mythen* 150; Hanisch 408). There has been some discussion about the reasons for this, and there are a number of cogent explanations. Paul Smith points out that the paradigmatic elements of the genre had multiplied by then, and the genre guidelines had broken down (46). Hembus adds that a new generation of directors, having grown up without Westerns, could not live up to the standards of auteur-Westerns of older directors with a certain relationship to the genre through their upbringing; and, in a sort of vicious cycle, actors could not grow into Western roles for the lack of a mass production (*Lexikon* 27). However, the most consideration has been given to the coincidence of Ronald Reagan's presidency and the decrease of Westerns in output and popularity, although the connection is interpreted in varying ways. Paul Smith and Hanisch see Reagan's neoconservative ideology of traditional American values as the perfect base for a Western revival, triggering at least the release of some films, but being suppressed by other factors (46; 408). On the other hand, Hembus argues that a former Western actor did harm to the credibility of a genre, which, moreover, is not necessarily communist, but somewhat skeptical about financial power and capitalism (*Lexikon* 26-7). In any case, the audience of the time did not want to see the pioneer myth being shattered as drastically as in *Heaven's Gate*, the biggest financial blow to the genre yet (Weidinger, *Nationale Mythen* 150; see above). This exposure of the American dream in an epic about a free country, which, however, has to be fought for in order to become the home of immigrants, is told from the perspective of a man who has achieved everything the American dream could promise, but looks back on his encounters with the poor social class, who built the country under dreadful strain (Hanisch 412; Grob and Kiefer 341). Here, the Western genre is made use of to bring the "unlived" and destroyed to the memory of the America of 1980, in exchange for the beautiful nostalgia (Grob and Kiefer 342). *Silverado* (1985) is always mentioned as the typical example for the eighties Western (probably for the lack of other examples): according to Hembus a deserved flop, which mixes traditional themes in the most naive way (*Lexikon* 26). Allegedly meant as a primer for the Western-deprived Generation X, it renounces the reflective view of revisionist Westerns, devotes itself to the mythic archetypes of the genre, and plays with its topoi while adjusting them to the aesthetics of the contemporary action-adventure film (Smith, Paul 47; Rauscher 343). Next to this stands one of Clint Eastwood's sporadic but continuous contributions to the genre, *Pale Rider*, of the same year. Relatively unaffected by the generational circumstances, Eastwood explained his motivation for making this financial success by an instinctive need to regularly create a Western, the root of American cinema and his own career (Smith, Paul 45, 48). With Eastwood's characteristic melancholy and skeptical view, *Pale Rider* presents an attractive modern analogy to *Shane* (1953), with a basically equal plot line, but essential variations that nevertheless underscore the films' similarities in their differences (Smith, Paul 49). So the character of Shane's admirer Joey, for example, is replaced by a girl, Megan, in *Pale Rider* (Smith, Paul 49). Apart from this variation on the Oedipal potential, the film raises issues of gender by turning the Western women's traditionally maintained objection towards violent behavior to complicity under the hand of the "mysterious stranger's" masculine power (Smith, Paul 50).[4] What both *Silverado* and *Pale Rider* share, as the predominant examples for the eighties Western, is an alleged "unabashed embrace of the values of the old Westerns," trying to persuade the audience that they "have never lost the simple and straightforward values of the mythic Old West. Look here, these films declaim, America is America again" (Smith, Paul 49).

Unforgiven, a revision of the genre without dispersion is the one Western of the early nineties which has enjoyed most consistent approval (Kiefer 353). The film presents a novel perspective on frontier violence, depicting the destructive reality and actual effects of violent acts, not the traditional ideological motivations and consequences of violence as most Westerns before, including Eastwood's own (Grist 297). *Unforgiven* implicates that the problem of violence deserves the prime focus in any debate on America's social order, and contextualized the contemporary violent climate effectively, although the screenplay (which Eastwood liked because in it killing is "demythologicalized, if such a word exists") was already written in the seventies (Grist 297; *Clint Eastwood*). The cruel torture of the African American character Ned by authorities, which ultimately results is his death, for example, parallels with the Rodney King court case of the time the film was released and the consequential L.A. riots (Grist 297; cf. Gale). The film scrutinizes the Wild West concept of justice, which various characters try to establish with the wrong motives and the wrong consequences, for the perpetrator as well as for the victim; their conflicting ideas of justice collide (Hembus, *Lexikon* 195; Grist 297). The ending, in which Eastwood's character becomes the "Ghost Rider" figure of *Shane* and his own former Westerns, has been criticized as excessive, but ultimately even the killings of his opponents are not heroic and leave open whether justice has been done or not (Kiefer 354; Hembus, *Lexikon* 195). Not at last this "most rigorous and thematically cohesive of the nineties Western" deconstructed Eastwood's own paradigmatic *Dirty Harry* image, and stood for him for the sum of all Westerns and action films he played in (Grist 294; *Clint Eastwood*).

The development of the Western hero

Actor, director, writer, and producer Gilbert M. Anderson is a well-remembered figure of the earliest period of Western cinema (Hanisch 29). Typically, his serial hero Broncho Billy is characterized as the "good bad man," an outlaw or misfit who proves humaneness in a borderline situation and is thus rehabilitated (Seeßlen and Weil 41). These films laid a noticeable foundation stone for the Western genre, as Broncho Billy served as a figure of identification for viewers, and by offering a moral which was part of most Westerns to come (Hanisch 28). Anderson's successor in popularity became William S. Hart, who played similar roles as that of Broncho Billy, but in less naive and linear films, and oriented towards a historical reality (Seeßlen and Weil 44). He established the character of the ambiguous Westerner, melancholic, lonesome, stoic, but dignified and firm; a hero by inner and outer compulsion, not by destiny

(Seeßlen and Weil 44-5). With Hart, who enjoyed great popularity from the mid-1910s to the early twenties, the Western began to be a genre prone to tragedy (Seeßlen and Weil 47).

The Gunfighter (1950), *Shane*, and *High Noon* are three trailblazing films of the fifties which each present an innovative and influential treatment of the Western hero. *The Gunfighter* is one of the first manifestations of the anti-hero, as the audience is made to sympathize with the morally most reprehensible character, an aging gunfighter who is challenged by a young, emulating follower (Parkinson and Jeavons 62-3). The rather conventional plot of *Shane* is compensated by its protagonist, who, fighting a fight which is not his, takes the shape of a mythological figure, almost unearthly, and allegorical for a protecting force behind the white settlement of the West (Seeßlen and Weil 124). *High Noon*, the epitome of the fifties Western, and famous for the political stance against McCarthyism it takes, features a hero whose Western moral forces him to act neither rationally nor exemplary, but only to maintain the values he has built his life upon (Parkinson and Jeavons 63; Seeßlen and Weil 123). These pathetic or unsentimental hero types share a psychology which unites a dented self-consciousness from past deeds with a wearing introspective and the inability to change their frontier ways (Seeßlen and Weil 126). This aspect of self-doubt was added to the formula of the Westerner in the fifties and was to be found in countless films from then on. *3:10 to Yuma* (1956) will be of special interest later; it shall only be mentioned here for its relevancy in continuing to de-heroize the Western protagonist, which even remained an exception at its time but was frequently taken up again in the seventies (Seeßlen and Weil 142). The protagonist in *3:10 to Yuma* becomes a hero through outer circumstances and utterly involuntarily and afterwards returns to his simple, unheroic life instead of becoming a living icon like conventional Western legends (Seeßlen and Weil 142).

The sixties introduced a new Western hero prototype: the cold, professional gunfighter, hardly capable of any human relation, a formula which was to be the core element of the Italian Western, the one "Western movement" outside of the US with the greatest impact (Seeßlen and Weil 162-4). Although this paper focuses on American Western productions, the Italian Western shall briefly be focused on here, rather for its supposed influence on the US Western, than for a recent trend to pay greater attention to "Spaghetti Westerns."[5] The Italian Western had its heyday between 1964, the release year of *A Fistful of Dollars*, and the early seventies; *Once Upon a Time in the West* (1968) has been called the artistic peak of the European Western (*DTV-Lexikon* 20: 50). Among the distinguishing features of the Italian Western, the most striking are the obsession with violence and the dry hero characters. The violent excesses of Italowesterns are notorious: violence here is no longer unavoidable, and is celebrated like an art (Seeßlen and Weil 182). And the prototypical Italowestern hero, as has been hinted above, is a cold, calculating professional, a "businessman," whose deeds are rewarded with money, not with moral goods (Seeßlen and Weil 182). However, he still possesses a trace of righteousness, which allows him to instinctively bring justice to a world he would rather avoid (Seeßlen and Weil 182). That the Italowestern's violence influenced Peckinpah strongly in making *The Wild Bunch* has been claimed by both of the most effective directors of Italian Westerns, Sergio Leone and Sergio Corbucci; but there is a difference in Peckinpah's purpose to show violence, which is to de-romanticize it, in contrast to its glorification (Frayling, *Spaghetti Westerns* 280-1). In other American films made in the aftermath of the Italians, the influence is undeniable--the best examples being Clint Eastwood's American Westerns, where he naturally brought in and digested his personal confrontation with the subgenre, and his character from Leone's "Dollar trilogy" (cf. Frayling, *Spaghetti Westerns* 281 ff.). As works of Clint Eastwood to come are to be considered of no small role in the later history of the American Western, the significance of the Italian Western shall be acknowledged here.

Pat Garret and Billy the Kid (1973) has been mentioned above, and exemplifies the pessimistic seventies in presenting heroes who do not want to be heroes anymore, and a dilapidated West, populated by cowardly masses, ruling criminals, and a few remnants from past days (Hanisch 384). While the sixties and the seventies were marked by the steadily opposing forces of John Wayne Westerns and liberal-left criticisms of directors like Arthur Penn or Robert Altman, most of both of those shared disenchantment with institutions and mainstream values of the American society (Lenihan 149). The heroes of these films were fascinating and frightening, but by no means figures of identification; their movement is almost always equated with an escape, and the seventies are generally seen as the end of the Western as such (Seeßlen and Weil 200-2; cf. Weidinger, *Nationale Mythen* 150).

Native Americans

The fifties announced a turnabout in the view of the Native American in the Western, who had rarely served as more than an atavistic, invisible threat before. A key film in the film industries' attitude towards the American Indian, *Broken Arrow* (1950), though flawed from a modern perspective, paved the way for following reassessments of the whites-Natives conflict (Parkinson and Jeavons 61-2). *Broken Arrow* and *Devil's Doorway* (1950) introduced two substantial themes in the "Indian-Western:" the difficult process of peacemaking next to the attempt of an individual integration of a member of the one party into the other, typically represented by a symbolical mixed marriage (Seeßlen and Weil 147-50). John Ford's grand *The Searchers* (1956) can not remain unmentioned, neither in an account of Western film history, nor in one of "Indian-Westerns" in particular.[6] This much recognized film has been called the most complex treatment of frontier racism and settlement and the "Moby Dick of the Western," and its bottom line is the sobering realization of the white protagonists that they are not the legitimate owners of the land, that the Natives are in the right, but that the anger of the whites, sprung from self-hate and despair, is the historically more powerful force (Seeßlen and Weil 157-9).

The characteristic parallels between American history and the present in the films of the sixties and seventies surfaced especially in Westerns with a Native American theme, where the Vietnam War found its mirror in the Indian Wars (Belton 291). The reawakening sympathy for Native Americans of the sixties found its peak in the still highly appreciated, in many aspects remarkable *Little Big Man*. If *The Wild Bunch* was the film to destroy a myth, *Little Big Man* was the one to partly revive it, through a subjective narrator who recounts history as he sees it, respectively, would like to see it, and recreates the myth of the West in a mixture of nostalgia and satire, while presenting the deepest understanding of Native Americans in the Western until then (Parkinson and Jeavons 86-9). Clint Eastwood's *The Outlaw Josey Wales* (1976), starring the same Indian lead, Chief Dan George, continues this approach, and Eastwood claimed to have chosen he script for its being "the first story which depicted Native Americans with a sense of humor" (*Clint Eastwood*).

In addition to that, it shall be mentioned that although Westerns as such were relatively rare in the eighties, the basic narrative patterns of the genre were still predominant in action-adventure films, with Western stories transferred into modern or future times (Weidinger, *Nationale Mythen* 246; Hanisch 408). *First Blood* (1981), which shows astonishing parallels to the neo-Western *Lonely Are the Brave* (1962), and is said to have been one of the favorite films of Ronald Reagan, embodies a new kind of Indian sympathy: the pursued protagonist's ancestry is noted by the local sheriff as part Indian, part German ("A hell of a combination," he remarks) and when left to rely on his primeval instincts to survive in the wilderness, he dresses up in a Native American style, brandishing an enormous knife (Belton 317). In the sequel, *Rambo: First Blood Part Two* (1985), the character would eventually boast a high-tech bow and arrow.

At the beginning of the nineties, the "eco-Western" *Dances With Wolves* enjoyed such a tremendous immediate success with audiences and critics that discussions thereafter have mainly focused on the film's faults, while taking its assets as obvious. These criticisms include such pointless contemplations as to whether this film is to be called a Western or not, besides more relevant aspects, like the rivalry between Lakota and Pawnee tribes resembling the stereotypical noble savage-bloodthirsty savage conflict, the implication at the end that the Lakota Sioux are now completely extinct, and it ultimately being another white view of Native Americans, and hence the white protagonist becoming a "better Indian than the Indians themselves" towards the end (Kilpatrick 124, 126, 130; Hembus, *Lexikon* 29, 126). So, in spite of the undeniably positive attempts of a meticulous depiction of Native Americans as human beings, or the authentic use of Indian languages, the opinions about the significance of *Dances With Wolves* are divided. Kilpatrick, for example, concludes that "though not perfect, this film deserves a few points" (130), whereas Jojola sees it as a bad copy of *Little Big Man*, which, other than the latter, "was apolitical and subconsciously plied its appeal by professing a simple New Age homily about peace and Mother Earth" (17). Jojola does not deny the impact of *Dances With Wolves*, which ushered forth a series of "Indian sympathy films"--for him, however, a term with negative connotations (17). Two other notable Westerns of the nineties, *Black Robe* (1991) and *Dead Man* (1995), are rather individualistic works and not as easy to be categorized; but they have a common Native American theme inherent, which underscores this alleged trend in the Western of the nineties.[7]

2.3. The Genre Today

So how is the Western genre faring since the year 2000? Without definite numbers and the decade not having come to a close yet, it is risky to make any conjectures about whether these years will produce a larger number of relevant Westerns in sum than, for example, the nineties. Listing a seemingly large number of Western made in or after 2000 in the following may create the illusion that this is the case, but obviously the paragraphs above presented only a selective choice of relevant films of each decade. On the other hand, the following account of the most recent films shall neither make any claims for completeness--but it may be noticed that a film was rather included than not; in fact, most films that I could find (and even some TV productions) which show a clear thematic or contextual relation to the Western genre and were released after 1999 will be mentioned at least briefly. My personal instinctive judgment, though, is that the average annual output of Hollywood Westerns since 2000 does not exceed that of the previous decade significantly, nor the other way round.

The notion of a "Western revival" shall therefore be treated carefully. Weidinger, who supports the opinion that the genre collapsed altogether in 1977, dismisses any speculations in that direction straight away (*Nationale Mythen* 150). He sees any successful and significant Westerns released between 1976 and 2005 as individual phenomena, and points out correctly that Clint Eastwood is the only exception of a director or actor devoting himself to the Western with continual artistically interesting results during that time, directing and starring in *The Outlaw Josey Wales*, *Pale Rider*, and *Unforgiven*, in addition to the half pro-Western, half Western parody *Bronco Billy* (1980) (Weidinger, *Nationale Mythen* 150). If there is any actor/director with a somewhat solid relation to the genre next to Eastwood, it may be Kevin Costner, who starred in four Westerns altogether (*Silverado*, *Dances With Wolves*, *Wyatt Earp* (1994), *Open Range*), directing two of them (*Dances With Wolves*, *Open Range*). It is true that this hardly compares with the prolific preoccupation with the genre of a John Ford, Anthony Mann, or Sam Peckinpah. However, a primary Western director is no prerequisite for a significant Western, as the example of *High Noon*'s Fred Zinneman proved, who went on to make only one more Western after this highly acclaimed debut. But even though Weidinger approves of the works of Eastwood and Costner, he does not acknowledge them as novel interpretations of the genre, but merely as continuations of the revisionist Westerns of the sixties and seventies--no inappropriate assumption when considering the parallels between *Dances With Wolves* and *Little Big Man*, or that the script of *Unforgiven* was written in the seventies (*Nationale Mythen* 151; see above). The dilemma seems to be that it is not possible to make a Western as they were done fifty years ago, for sociocultural reasons which make writers and directors rack their brains (Weidinger, *Nationale Mythen* 151). Then again, apart from a number of films Weidinger does not mention, some larger Western productions have been released after the publication of his account, with considerable success among audiences as well as critics. The following list will aim to introduce the greatest part of major Western releases or films closely connected to the genre since the year 2000, before four examples will be picked out for closer examination and with regard to the issues introduced above, in the next chapter.

Shanghai Noon (2000) is a Jackie Chan film set in the Wild West, rather than a Western starring Jackie Chan. This action comedy relies on the latter's trademark of fast-paced, well-choreographed stunts and his comical talent, and can not offer more to the genre than its immediate precursors, later Western comedies like *Back to the Future III* (1990) (from which it takes the comical play on the names of actual Western stars) or *Maverick* (from which it takes the humor of men taking a bath in the same room). Likewise aimed at young, supposedly Western-uninitiated viewers, it contents itself with spoofs of the most familiar Western stereotypes, the few remnants that such an audience is expected to be familiar with. Its sequel, *Shanghai Knights* (2003), set in Victorian England, underscores that the successful concept depends rather on the actor stars than the Western context. The few admittedly well-photographed landscapes and attractive set-pieces, therefore, are not sufficient to place *Shanghai Noon* among "serious attempts to grapple once again with the traditions of the Western" (Grist 294). However, Kitses rehabilitates it somewhat as "following the venerable example of earlier Hollywood comics going West" (*Horizons West* 5).

Four noticeable films were released in the next years; two of those, *Open Range* (2003) and *The Missing* (2003), deserve special attention and will be dealt with in detail in the next chapter. Categorizing the other two, *Gods and Generals* (2002) and *Cold Mountain* (2003), as Westerns is not wholly unproblematic, because both are actually Civil War dramas. But though not literally set in the West, such films are still favorably included as Western, since the West's prosperity was of interest to the war faring parties, and the outcome of the War in turn shaped the West significantly (Hembus, *Geschichte* 241). Classics such as *Shenandoah* (1964), for example, are always quoted as Westerns.[8] As Civil War films do not seem to be rare among the cinematic history of America, the release of *Gods and Generals* arises the question what novelties this film might offer (Buscombe, *Gods* 51). Apparently none worth mentioning apart from its notable visual authenticity, as this large-scale epic account of three Southern victories incorporates the paradigmatic sympathy for the South, obscure interpretations of patriotism, and ideological tendencies full of pathos, but no lessons about the wider course of the war, and not more than a naive and sentimental equivocation of the slavery problem (Buscombe, *Gods* 51). In his review of *Gods and Generals*, Sharrett fervently criticizes the depiction of African Americans as inarticulate, subservient servants and slaves, accepting their fate with endurance (38). *Cold Mountain*, on the other hand, offers less conventional aspects. Basically condemning the War, and again looking at it from a Southern perspective, it contrasts views of all kinds of parties, with the bottom line being the absurdity and irrationality of war, and that a different uniform is not what makes an enemy. In the opening battle scene, a black Union soldier and a Native American Confederate confront each other, hesitating for a short moment of realization that they are both fighting a war that is not theirs. Most of the film is told from the perspective of the women left behind, who can not make much sense of the war. When the news of it arrive and the town's men start out of the church to cheer and celebrate, the women's critical reserve lets the viewer estimate their rational instinct clearly higher than the men's for the first time. The male protagonist whom the viewer sympathizes with is practically a deserter, and consequently the (Southern) home guard becomes the true enemy of the (Southern) protagonists. But although one member of the former gets the minimal opportunity to present his viewpoint, he is principally bad, as the rest of his henchmen, and this black-and-white depiction is one fault of the film. And so are the supernatural elements (the female protagonist sees her future when looking down a well with a mirror), which do not help much to get rid of the sentimental touch. At the back of this, *Cold Mountain* does not ignore the specific politics of the American Civil War, but has a wider significance, as the protagonist's desertion is "not a protest against the Southern cause but the result of a profound war-weariness" (Buscombe, "The Homecoming" 32). However, McCrisken and Pepper see this indecisive ambivalence as a major fault and undermine *Cold Mountain*'s significance as a historical film: of the three ways in which a film can make the past meaningful--by visioning, contesting or revisioning history--this film achieves only the first but fails in the latter two (83).

2004 followed with a film not set within the immediate core of the Wild West's temporal boundaries as well, but worth mentioning as a remake of the directional debut of the Western's most prominent star, John Wayne. *The Alamo* (1960) was not received as well as Wayne was hoping, and the same was true of its reprise (Hembus, *Lexikon* 35-6; Weidinger,

Nationale Mythen 152). With the Alamo theme being a classic example of American historical iconography, twisting the role of white America in the conquest of the West by depicting a heroic battle of "underdog" bringers of freedom and democracy against a predominant fascist power, Buscombe asks for the purpose in making the 2004 *Alamo*, as there is little new in this version of the story (*Alamo* 54; cf. Hembus, *Lexikon* 104-110). The only exception seems to be the portrayal of American folk legend Davy Crockett "as a complex character--half clown, half canny politician, well aware of the ironies of being a legend in his own lifetime" (Buscombe, *Alamo* 54).

More of a Western in character, and set at the right time, but not the conventional place, is the Australian Western *The Proposition* (2004), which handles the frontier history of the British colony in a way which might be wished for more often in American Westerns. While the parallels and contrasts between Australian and American "Westerners" have often been the reason for jokes, as in the lighthearted comedy Western *Lightning Jack* (1994), the actual white settlement of Australia surely corresponds with the American frontier history in a great many aspects. Not at last, Native and African Americans have a sort of common counterpart in the aboriginal population of the southern continent, an evocative which *The Proposition* duly emphasizes by featuring aboriginal scouts and servants employed by British authorities, depictions of white maltreatment and oppression of captured Aborigines, and a white perception of warlike Aborigines as the mysterious, unapproachable, feral threat of the Heart of Darkness of the Outback (Fig. 4). Director John Hillcoat apparently put a lot of effort in researching the complex relationship between the aboriginal population and white settlers, and these attempts at historicity, underscored by the juxtaposition of historical photographs and stills trimmed as such in the opening credits, are probably also the reason for the film's extreme violence (Roddick 29). Although script writer Nick Cave subordinated such claims of authenticity to efforts of giving the film a poetical quality in contrasting human violence with the beauty of the landscape, the director repeatedly stresses that nineteenth-century Australia was in fact a very violent period (Roddick 29).[9] And while the makers underlined the "Australianess" of *The Proposition* by featuring an exclusively Australian cast, they did not deny the noticeable strong influence of Anthony Mann and Sam Peckinpah, apart from a resemblance of the main character to that of Leone's "Dollar trilogy" (Roddick 28-9). In this sense, and as it "cleverly [entwines] Australia's colonial history with the Western's mythic structure of betrayal and revenge," the significance of *The Proposition* among the Westerns of recent years must not be overlooked (Spencer).

Fig. 4. *The Proposition.*

One of the most archetypal Westerns of recent years, both with respect to its setting and narrative structure, remained relatively little noticed. In the thrilling revenge Western *Seraphim Falls* (2006), about the settlement of accounts between Civil War veterans, the story line follows the "battle of wits" between a vengeance-seeking pursuer and a crafty survivor, with the balance of power constantly changing until the showdown, which follows a flashback sequence that enlightens the viewer about the past events that caused the conflict (Buscombe, *Seraphim*). It features a range of typical Western elements, landscapes, and themes, yet it offers attractive and unobtrusive variations to common patterns. Although it is set in practically the whole scope of available Western landscapes in succession, starting out in snowy mountainous forests of the Rocky Mountains, followed by stretching pine forests, plains, savanna, steppe, and ending up in salt-flats as the pursuit takes its course, they take on an allegorical function beyond the usual extent.[10] In *Seraphim Falls*, as the landscape gets more and more barren, it mirrors the viewer's perception of the relationship between pursuer and pursued and their motives and personalities, which gain clarity in the course of the narration. The distractions of unevenness and vegetation are lost bit by bit, just as the main characters get devoid of fur coats, companions, jackets, equipment, hats, and horses by and by, until they face each other in the flat, far-stretching desert, and nothing remains but two guns, two bullets, and two men, their clothes now finally reflecting the true moral alignment: the pursued, with whom the viewer sympathized all along, turned out to be the bad guy and wears dark tones, the pursuer, the one that harm has really been done to by the killing of his wife and child, in bright tones. The landscape, the men's appearance, and the conflict get down to the essentials. But the flashback sequence, which has uncovered these terms, and is positioned just before the culmination of events in tradition of Sergio Leone, also suggests that the true fault is to be found in the War. The pursuer forgives the pursued and thus settles the account, and both walk off in different directions. In spite of various faults Buscombe finds with the film, such as the irrational involvement of secondary characters, and its inability to achieve wider anti-war resonances (*Seraphim*), *Seraphim Falls* maintains a steadfast position among newer Westerns as a notable juxtaposition of traditional elements with unconventional structural and formulaic innovations.

Most recently, in 2007, two films created a stir among those interested in the Western, and perhaps caused some cautious optimism of a renaissance. The remake of the fifties classic *3:10 to Yuma* and the novel perspective on the Jesse James saga *The Assassination of Jesse James by the Coward Robert Ford* have already proved notable representations of the genre in the short time of their existence. Therefore they will be treated in detail in the next chapter. A number of other films have not been mentioned yet, but deserve special attention as well. Several films have been released in recent years that resist a distinct categorization as Westerns primarily by their time of setting. Although not all are strictly post-Westerns, the relevancy of *All the Pretty Horses* (2000), *Brokeback Mountain* (2005) and *The Three Burials of Melquiades Estrada* (2005) to the genre shall nevertheless be considered.

All the Pretty Horses is first and foremost a faithful adaptation of the novel of the same name by Cormac McCarthy, "the creator of a high-art Western literature far from the pulps of a Louis L'Amour" (Buscombe, *Horses*; Kitses, "Bloodred" 13). As a film, this post World War II initiation story of young cowboys, set along the Mexican border, has been called a neo- and existential Western, with the director claiming *The Searchers* and *High Noon* as influential models (Kitses, "Bloodred" 13). In sum, this film seems to be another example of the unification of deconstructive elements with Western nostalgia; this time, though, with the former as the predominant half. The nostalgic elements are the frontier iconography, the emphasis on horses, a hide-and-seek shootout, the regret of the male protagonists to have been born into a time when the frontier was history, and their wish to retrieve Western values by becoming old-time cowboys, the youngest of them showing off his gun-handling skills much as we would imagine Billy the Kid do. The deconstructive elements are the anachronisms of the above due to the film's setting, and the episodic structure, which "undercuts genre and narrative conventions" (Kitses, "Bloodred" 14). Kitses, who suspects the subject matter to be related to Sam Peckinpah's thematic interests, sees McCarthy's literary model, and consequently the film, as a creative voice to contemporary revisionist historical studies, which see the West as conquest, savagery and exploitation ("Bloodred" 13). In that sense, in spite of its distance from the genre at first sight, *All the Pretty Horses* might provide a revealing insight into present-day attitudes towards the Western genre.

Probably most widely recognized among the pro-Westerns of recent years has been *Brokeback Mountain*, raising awareness to homosexual issues and elaborating on the image of the gay cowboy. Thus it shall not be mentioned here for its narrative structure, which is hardly Western typical (except for some showdown-reminiscent scenes of confrontations in modern environments like supermarkets (Gilbey 50)), but for its deconstruction of a common Western paradigm by exposing the homosexual connotations of male companionship. The associative link between latent homosexuality and the iconic motif of the cowboy, which has proved fruitful in the great attendance of rodeo events organized and frequented exclusively by "gay cowboys" in recent years, is actually existent since at least the fifties (Hembus, *Lexikon* 397; *Spiel mir das Lied*). Buscombe calls *Brokeback Mountain* "only the latest in a long tradition of Westerns to explore the intense, unspoken and physical bonds between its two male heroes" and investigates seemingly conventional Westerns for their homosexual implications ("Man to Man" 34). The relative insignificance of women characters, the Western's inherent hyper-masculinity, and the coincidence of the genre's decline with the rising social acceptance of homosexuality in the early sixties, support these propositions (Buscombe, "Man to Man" 34). Buscombe provides a collage of Westerns through cinematic history which feature such patterns of intricate male "buddy" companionship that allow a reading in terms of subliminal homosexuality: *My Darling Clementine* (1946), *Ride the High Country* (1961), *Butch Cassidy and the Sundance Kid* (1969), *Monte Walsh* (1970), and also the recent *Open Range* ("Man to Man"). While the credit of making explicit use of these potentialities for the first time does also not go to *Brokeback Mountain*, but to Andy Warhol's grotesque *Lonesome Cowboys* (1968), the former must be noted for the more presentable reconsideration of these issues, which has not at last found remarkably wide resonance (Hembus, *Lexikon* 397-8).

The Three Burials of Melquiades Estrada, Tommy Lee Jones' debut as a director, has been noticed with regard to various aspects, the connection to the Western genre being not the prime one. Attempts to classify it have resulted in a categorization of simply belonging to a group of films exploring the world of the border ("too few to constitute a genre"), a dismissal as grotesque dark comedy, and an equation to William Faulkner's *As I Lay Dying*, with its theme of transporting a deceased to the burial place of his final wish under arduous strains (Buscombe, *Three Burials*; Kitses, "Days of the Dead" 15; Smith, Grahame). Buscombe reservedly counts only the horseback journey, the revenge theme, and a tradition of cross-border exploration as Western elements (*Three Burials*), and Jones himself has initially disclaimed the Western label of *The Three Burials*, but eventually accepted the term "contemporary Western" (Kitses, "Days of the Dead" 18). Regardless of this skepticism it has been seen in a Western context, not at last because of Jones' associations with the genre, somewhat exaggeratedly compared to the roles of John Wayne and Gary Cooper by Kitses ("Days of the Dead" 18). Although *The Three Burials* suggests a tendency towards art film-like realizations in the recent Western, it is at the same time an example for the unfailing creative potentiality of the themes and iconography, and even as a reformation it is evidence for the Western's versatility as such (Kitses, "Days of the Dead" 18).

It might seem imprudent to mention Western feature films and television Westerns in one breath, but one of the latter shall be mentioned again here, at least for its great popular success, which has been read as proof for the genre's enduring appeal and audience acceptance (Kitses, "Days of the Dead" 18; Drysdale 136).[11] *Deadwood* (2004-6) is mostly set in the historical town of Deadwood, and blends fictional characters and events with its idea of historical ones (see above). Wild Bill Hickock appears as a heroic, but contemplative figure, and Calamity Jane as a lovable rogue. But the greatest efforts in historicity have been put by the makers into the town set-piece, which startlingly bears comparison with nineteenth-century photographs of the actual Deadwood. In its intricate detail, however, the art design ultimately equals authenticity with filth, in the town's muddy roadways (which let those of *Dead Man*'s Machine shine through), the people's shabby clothes, their manners, and, especially, their language. Only the series' male protagonist (as generally the most archetypal Western character, he is the one which comes closest to being the "hero") conforms to what Tompkins has called the genre's "not-language," a masculine demonstration of control over emotion by not speaking, as Peter Schwenger describes it (55; qtd. in Tompkins 56). Most of the other characters are identified by the wealth of their foul-mouthed vocabulary: a corrupt Chinese communicates with the Anglo population only via the one English word in his repertoire, "cocksucker;" Calamity Jane speaks fluently, but relies largely on that one word as well; and the language of the town's supposed sympathetic villain Al Swearengen is best to be inferred by his name. Thus trying to correct the myth of the West's taciturn language and replacing it by one of profanity, and making similar claims of presenting a "truer" image of the pioneer era (which basically only adjusts to the preferences of a young generation of viewers raised on rap music), *Deadwood* depicts a romanticized West according to contemporary notions of imperfection. Not at last, its characters are allegories of deficiency; most villains have vulnerable sides and their bad traits are explained by past traumas, and the protagonists embody human frailty. However, the overall tendency of the series is optimistic, and this curious mixture of popularized elements, deconstruction, and its claim for authenticity have not only earned *Deadwood* a huge fan base and cult status, but also attention by critics and scholars. O'Hehir reads it as a significant allegory of late capitalism, "about the collision between the professed ideals of America and the often ruthless reality," and the series has produced a collection of scholarly essays that dissect *Deadwood* in terms of psychoanalysis, gender theory, sociology and others (*Reading Deadwood*, edited by David Lavery).

Though not for ever, this list of newer Westerns could go on for a while when including popularizations like the comic-book adaptation *Blueberry* (2004), other successful television series like *Into the West* (2005), or *Broken Trail* (2006), or more films along the blurred boundaries of post- and pro-Westerns, like *There Will Be Blood* (2007) or *No Country For Old Men* (2007). However, although this might add up to a stately collection of titles, the absolute number of significant productions within the genre's narrower contextual guidelines would remain comparatively small. While this speaks rather against a second coming of the Western, the question remains whether the available films of later years are part of a common movement, a new Western wave so to say, or merely a resumption of the revisionist films of the sixties and seventies, as Weidinger suggests (*Nationale Mythen* 150). Neither is the possibility of a delayed continuation of the trends set by Eastwood and Costner in the early nineties to be waved aside, especially when considering the latter's *Open Range.* In an attempt to answer this question, the cinematic and narrative elements of contemporary Westerns must be examined in relation to those of the "classic" formula Western, but also to revisionist Westerns of later periods. To determine this relative distance to their predecessors, the following analysis of example films will concentrate chiefly on two aspects, which I have termed deconstruction and nostalgia. These two features may be understood as the opposite ends of a spectrum, with deconstruction marking any deviation from conventional genre forms (at present rather more likely), and nostalgia any unexpected approximation to these traditional forms, or even a romanticizing of the frontier as a historical and mythical period, if perhaps in a wistful manner, but obviously motivated by a longing for obsolete values and customs.

3. The Recent Western in Four Examples

Even if any speculations about a recent Western "wave," "revival," or even "comeback" were aimed at, those were not to be based solely on the overall number of releases, but primarily on the number of "significant productions," as I have called them in the last chapter, meaning artistically and film-historically outstanding films. The criteria for such is naturally not as indicative as simple figures, and one easily runs the risk of over- or underrating certain films, rooted in personal biases. Therefore, it seems sensible to rely on a balance of judgments by scholars, critics, award committees, and not at last the broad public, next to one's own discernment. Films like *Stagecoach* (1939), *High Noon* (1952), *The Wild Bunch* (1969) or *Unforgiven* (1992), for instance, have proved relatively steadfast against any questioning of their significance. Even if the films dealt with in this chapter may not turn out such landmarks, they have all met with critical praise and scholarly attention. Kitses calls *Open Range* (2003) "[b]y far the most impressive Western since *Unforgiven*" (*Horizons West* 7) and *The Assassination* (2007) "a poetic masterpiece, a landmark in the genre and an extraordinary Western" ("Twilight" 16). Macnab finds the characters and themes in James Mangold's *3:10 to Yuma* (2007) "as fresh as ever." Weidinger praises the depiction of the female protagonist in *The Missing* (2003), and generally approves of all four films (*Nationale Mythen* 152-3; "Re: 'Nationale Mythen'"). *Open Range* is the only exception of only mediocre box office success among the four, and both *3:10 to Yuma* and *The Assassination* have earned Academy Award nominations, the latter eventually scoring two wins; a rarity in the Western genre (cf. Grist 294). But, as especially *The Missing* has also faced some negative critiques, critical and commercial success were not the only criteria in the selective choice presented here. So, these four films complement each other well in covering most of the relevant aspects in a genre-specific discussion with regard to the present time. All of them deal with forms of frontier violence, and more specifically, *Open Range* takes up the cowboy-rancher theme, *The Missing* deals with cultural contact between Native Americans and whites, *3:10 to Yuma* scrutinizes Western moral and heroism, and *The Assassination* investigates outlawry and one of the flamboyant legends of the West, Jesse James, in questioning the relation between Western fact and fiction. Each film, but most significantly *3:10 to Yuma*, leans on established Western classics; *The Assassination* allows for a comparison with former treatments of a popular myth, and *The Missing* is notable for its reflections on gender in the genre. Hence, if any choice of a sensible number of films can be appropriate to cover a thorough analysis of the Western genre at the present time, it must be these four. It has been suggested above that these films shall especially be correlated to the classic formula Western--not only a helpful, but a crucial task. While a universally applicable definition of the formula Western is hard to search for (for example, are films like *Shane* (1953) and *High Noon* instances of the Western formula in its purest form, or, as André Bazin and Robert Warshow criticized, do they bear content outside the traditional themes and unnecessary aestheticizing (qtd. in Kitses, *Horizons West* 3)?), this paper will mainly rely on the work of a pioneer in the field of Western genre theory, John G. Cawelti's *The Six-Gun Mystique*, to approach the concept of the "classic" Western.

3.1. *Open Range*: A Formulaic Western

Open Range tells the story of two cowboys, old-timer Boss Spearman (Robert Duvall) and the silent Charley Waite (Kevin Costner), who free-graze their cattle on the open range in 1882. The other members of their outfit are the thickset, simpleminded Mose, and the adolescent Chicano Button. When Mose is sent back to a town they passed to pick up supplies and does not return, Boss and Charlie follow him after to find out he has got into a fight and been jailed. "Mose don't start no fights," Boss assures the marshal, but although he seems to have given as good as he got, Mose is badly damaged. Boss and Charley get the message of the rancher and town's dictator Denton Baxter, who ordered the attack and arrest of Mose as a warning against the loathed free-grazers. He lets them go with a threat and an ultimatum to leave the area, and they let Mose be stitched up at the local doctor Walter Barlow and what seems to be his wife, Sue (Annette Bening). Back on the range the next day, they spot a group of masked riders in the distance, obviously Baxter's men. These let themselves be seen, but avoid a close encounter by riding off. Charley and Boss decide that offense is the best defense, leave Mose and Button behind with the cattle and wagon, and surprise the gunmen at night at their campfire, mangling and humiliating them. When they return, another troop of Baxter's henchman have attacked their partners, killing Mose and Charley's dog and hurting Button badly. Charley convinces Boss to return to town for medical attendance for Button. Mose and the dog are buried the next day and they head for the settlement, where Sue looks to Button's injuries, since the Doctor is out. Charley and Boss confront the marshal in the cafe, where they threaten to take law into their own hands. A violent conflict seems to be in the coming. Back at the doctor's house, they do not accept Sue's offer of a room for the night, but still pass the night there,

Boss mainly attending Button, and Charley falling asleep in his chair. The following day in the saloon, they learn about the townspeople's reserved attitude toward vigilantism, and that Sue is really Doctor Barlow's sister, not his wife. With the help of livery stable owner Percy's hints, they manage to outwit, capture, and imprison the marshal and his deputies, to have their back free for the coming confrontation with Baxter's army and hired professional gunmen. By the next morning, Charley and Sue have eventually got closer, and Boss advises Charley to say goodbye to her properly as they head for the showdown, since she might never again see him alive. Again with the help of Mack, they make their way through the chaotic gunfight, in which Boss is shot and most of Baxter's men get killed. After the involvement of Sue, the recovering Button, and several townspeople, Baxter is killed by Boss. This conflict over, Charley sends for Sue to meet him in the saloon alone, where their love for each other is suggested. But he tells her he will not be able to settle in this town peacefully, for his violent past and recent deeds. Charley rides out of town. However, he returns shortly, confesses Sue his love, proposes to her, and she accepts. Boss tells Charley of his definite plans to take over a saloon nearby and leave the cattle business, and decides for Charley to become his partner. The film ends with Charley, Sue, Button, and Boss looking forward to a bright future.

Open Range has been criticized as another product of Kevin Costner's egotism, but several aspects dismiss any notions of it being an archetypal "Costner film" and a simple continuation of former Western projects he has been involved in (Kitses, "Forgiven" 24). Not only does Costner allow Robert Duvall considerable screen presence and lends his own character ambivalence, but it will be seen that, as a Western, *Open Range* is a long way from *Dances With Wolves*, for example--and not only because the action involves not a single Native American (Kitses, "Forgiven" 24). Nevertheless a rather personal project, it proves the "continuing relevance and dynamic potential" of the Western and the director's serious loyalty to the genre (Kitses, *Horizons West* 7, 9). Lenihan argues that there is no reason for the Western to be less appropriate for today's audience than yesterday's (176), and it seems that Costner took this to heart, digging the genre up from the dirt on his very own, as Charley does in the beginning of the film with their wagon to get it going again (Fig. 5). When he is finally helped, it is by Mose, someone who respects Charley for defending him in spite of others' doubts about the profitability of his employment: an allegory of Costner's belief and engagement in a seemingly unpopular and risky genre. The basic striking characteristic of *Open Range* is its abandonment of revisionist norms in exchange for tried-and-true Western material (Kitses, *Horizons West* 7). The film does deliberately not pretend to redefine the genre or claim new innovations, but is traditionalist in depicting a conflict which has been seen a hundred times before (Weidinger, *Nationale Mythen* 152). The result shall be examined in the following, first with regard to its settings, characters and action pattern (the three fundamental factors of the Western formula as Cawelti sees them), before some aspects of violence, ethnicity, and deconstruction will be considered in what Kitses calls a "triumphant return to the classical Western" ("Forgiven" 24).

Fig. 5. *Open Range.*

To start with the setting, Costner obviously chose one of the most prototypical Western settings, the open range, neatly symbolizing the conflict between old, nostalgic values of individual cowboys, and the institutionalizing progress of organized ranchers. Also the date of the narration is clearly within the boundaries of the Wild West, although closer to its ending than its beginning: 1882. The wide, majestic, unspoiled landscape as the natural home of the heroes is complemented by the Western town embodying civilization; a contrast, as Buscombe notices, clearly favoring the former (*Open Range*), which is beautifully photographed in various shades of colorful light and celebrated with extensive shots. When Cawelti wrote of the characteristic openness of the Western landscape enabling a visually strong contrast between wilderness and society, he could not have wished for a better example than *Open Range* (43). When Boss and Charley ride into town for the first time, their looks keep a critical distance, as point-of-view shots depict their first impressions. In spite of the relative squalidness and tightness, and its busy crowd, town life has a sense of harmony at first, with kids playing, and men and women going about their business between the neatly detailed houses. But then two dark figures on the balcony of a storefront saying "barbed wire" in red letters indicate the threat to the heroes' way of life which lies in advancing civilization, and this is reflected in the music accompanying the scene, which ends on a threatening note after its harmonious beginning (The function of barbed wire as the allegorical threat of institutionalized cattle business to the Westerner's values is also indicated in the scene where the protagonists encounter Baxter's men as dark figures on a distant hill: a long shot of them riding towards the aggressors is disturbed by an ugly piece of ragged barbed wire dividing the frame). A tension between landscape and town, inherent to the Western (Tompkins 85), is made aware by *Open Range* as blatantly as no other Western could. The procedure in which Tompkins summarizes the relationship between the hero and the settlement is exactly that which we witness here:

> "The men go there to get supplies, [...] for respite and refuge. [...] Town is a magnet; it draws people. [...] But in fact, town always threatens to entrap the hero in the very things the genre most wishes to avoid: intimacy, mutual dependence, a network of social and emotional responsibilities." (86)

Note that the cowboys in *Open Range* are repeatedly drawn against their will to a town they had actually already passed, and this ultimately entangles them in the latter mentioned responsibilities above, mainly through the female protagonist Sue. The house of Sue and her brother, by the way, is not only singled out among the buildings by its location slightly apart from the town's core; the sky blue paint, the white picket fence, and the vegetable garden underscore the notion of domesticity it imposes on Charley, an inviting alternative of the else unwelcoming town settlement. Cawelti also treats the costume under the heading of setting, describing the formulaic cowboy dress, and, among other aspects, the simplest function of costume as a symbol for moral opposition (44-45). Although this film hardly makes use of such oversimplified patterns, one thing may be pointed out here. The character of Charley, being played by Kevin Costner, whose career repeatedly saw roles with a great emphasis on costume, is made visually prominent by his rather pointed hat, a shape which has hardly been seen in Westerns of recent years, at least not worn by the hero. It can even be argued that this shape of hat has not been considered fashionable with Western protagonists for several decades. However, in earlier days on the genre, this particular kind of hat was frequently seen--a fact which might underscore Costner's desire to return to the roots of the genre (Fig. 6).

Fig. 6. Left: Kevin Costner as Charley Waite in *Open Range.* Center: William S. Hart in *The Gunfighter* (1917), directed by himself. Still (from Parkinson and Jeavons 15). Right: Tom Mix. Publicity photo, c. 1920 (from Parkinson and Jeavons 16).

Cawelti suggests a triangle relationship between the characters of a classic Western, and it will be seen that most of the patterns he introduces can be found in *Open Range* as well. The three character groups in a Western are the townspeople; the outlaws or savages, as Cawelti calls them, i.e. the antagonist force; and at last the hero (40). There are prototypical townspeople in *Open Range*, including the freighter and his sons, the general store owner, Percy, and, most significantly, Sue. The villains are Baxter and his men, which includes Marshal Poole and his deputies, and the gunfighter Butler. In spite of Boss' omnipresence it is really Charley who fits the hero character pattern, and the former has to be seen as the secondary, but crucial role of the hero's companion. To begin with the townspeople, Saunders points out in his investigation of *Shane*, a Western with one of the most classical plots (if deliberately so), that the society must be weak enough to require the involvement of the hero (22). This is indeed the case here, where the settlers do not dare to step up to the tyrannical Baxter: "I didn't raise my boys to see them get killed," the freighter tells Charley. This, however, has led to the problem of the genre that it does not want to depict ordinary American citizens as cowardly and ineffectual (Saunders 22). The problem is solved here in the essential support the townspeople give Boss and Charley in the final gun battle (upon returning from seeking shelter in the church at first), according to Kitses a simple, pleasure providing solution in contrast to *High Noon*'s and Eastwood's preaching or "empowering" alternatives (*Horizons West* 8). However, their "support" is hardly more than that: when the store owner eventually makes use of his shotgun to fire at a gunman in ambush, he does not wound him--but Charley is made aware of the pursuer and manages to get the drop on him: still it is the hero who has to do the dirty work of the killing. One function of the classic plot as Will Wright defines it in *Sixguns and Society* (again in principle that of *Shane*), is the incomplete acceptance of the hero by society, a similar sort of resentment for him as it harbors for the villains (qtd. in Saunders 26). Such a tendency is soon counteracted by Boss' and Charley's sincere appearance and good deeds (they save a man's puppy from drowning), but it is there. The one citizen who is on their side from the beginning is the owner of the livery stable, Percy, who fits a particular group of townspeople characters perfectly. Cawelti sees these as a combination of the ambiguities of civilization which appear in the conflict between hero and settlers, typically Easterners having fled West, somehow alienated from the townspeople and therefore better able to feel with the hero (50). Percy takes on one of the important plot roles of this group, that of providing "sympathy and assistance to the hero at a crucial time" (Cawelti 50). While he may not necessarily be a fled Easterner, his past somewhat parallels with the hero's destiny. After he has kept the backs of the protagonists in the final shootout, and fired off some shots himself, we find out that it is not the first time he is in such a fight. But "it has been a while," as he tells them; he is out of practice, gets injured, and consequently "cannot function on the hero's ground [since he lacks] his skills in violence" (Cawelti 50). As the representative of this character group, Percy serves as a foil to the hero, and mediates between him and the town (Cawelti 51).

Fig. 7. *Open Range.*

However, the essential feature of the town is that there are women in it (Cawelti 47). Since the sexist tendencies of the Western genre have been seen as one of the major reasons for its decline in popular acceptance (cf. Weidinger, *Nationale Mythen* 154; see above), it is worth looking at how *Open Range* tackles the gender issue in as liberal a time as the present is considered to be. In casting a female lead over 40 in Annette Bening as Sue and making no secret of it (one might accuse *Johnny Guitar* (1953) of doing so by Joan Crawford's heavy makeup--she was 47 when that film was made (Hembus, Lexikon 346)), the film makes an important step away from inopportune Hollywood clichés, and Buscombe approves of this (*Open Range*). A shot of her brother in the foreground, saying goodbye to Boss and Charley after their first visit to their house, and Sue in the background, much closer to the building, deliberately suggests an "Angel-of-the-House" status, only to dissolve it later (Fig. 7). Several following scenes try to convince the viewer of the independence, individuality, and unusual resoluteness of Sue's character that the men tend to underrate. Boss, who stresses that he wants to see Button "looked after proper" and doubts the woman's competence in standing in for the absent doctor, is taken aback when Sue proves she knows very well what she is doing and indicates that he better not tell her how to do her job. Generally diffident, though, she gets a chance to stand her ground in the shootout, where she bravely intervenes to save Button (and in the course of doing so slaps the corrupt marshal--possibly a nod at *Dances With Wolves*' Stands-With-a-Fist). However, other than in *High Noon*, the woman's efforts are insufficient, and it is Charley who has to save her life in the end. So, Sue's character eventually fulfills all the traditional functions: a primary symbol for civilization, sexual fascination for the hero, and a relationship with the latter that reflects the ambiguities of the love, domesticity, and opportunity for the creation of a family the town offers, in contrast to the masculine honor and camaraderie of the wilderness life (Cawelti 47-9). One break with conventions can be noticed when she shows understanding for the hero "doing what he has to do," that is, facing the villains in a fatal confrontation (Kitses, "Forgiven" 26). Initially, she disapproves of the violent behavior of Boss and Charley in a manner more familiar to the genre (at one time, for example, she confronts Boss in a shot which makes them direct opposites in the contrasting color of costume and corresponding background (Fig. 8)--a scene which foreshadows how she will eventually take over Boss' role as a companion to Charley, as the formula requires (Cawelti 63)). That she ceases to do so later is an untypical development in her character, which, however, can obviously not be read as a significant advance towards an emancipation of the Western's woman. Presumably, Costner shares Saunders' view that the rare films with women in strong roles, like *Johnny Guitar*, "risk being dismissed as ludicrous, somehow not really westerns" (16), which determined his decisions about the characterization of Sue.

Fig. 8. *Open Range.*

The villain character group in *Open Range*, as opposed to the townspeople and the hero (Cawelti's terms "savages" and "outlaws" do both not seem appropriate here), is more or less made up of stock characters: a corrupt sheriff, Poole; a rancher-villain, Baxter; and a professional, but evil gunfighter, Butler. Only the balance of power between those is somewhat untypical, with Butler, whom one might expect to serve as the main antagonist to the hero, playing only a minor role. Relics of the basic traits of the villain are established in him; his dark, elegant dandy clothes contrast with Charley's simple attire, and when Butler laughs heartily at the marshal and deputies having been locked up by their common enemy, the scene cautiously suggests the often discernible friendship or respect between hero and villain (cf. Saunders 30). But his rather late actual appearance in the action and abrupt death by a head shot from Charley, which opens the showdown, render him an insignificant character. On the other hand, the rancher Baxter might be imagined to be only one evil representative of the town population, symbolizing the negative side of civilization (Cawelti 51). However, he is the most prominent and powerful villain in *Open Range* and thus serves as the main antagonist. His character in itself, though, corresponds to the usually less prominent paradigmatic figure of what Cawelti calls the banker- or rancher-villain:

> "In him, the pioneer goal of building a good society in the wilderness has become avarice and greed for individual wealth and power. Instead of the pioneer's mutual respect and loyalty, the banker-villain possesses skill

at manipulating and exploiting the townspeople to his own advantage." (51)

Significantly, Buscombe compares Baxter to the rancher Ryker in *Shane* and similar roles, underscoring Costner's devotion to the classic Western (*Open Range*). As with Ryker, there is a certain ambiguity about Baxter's ambition which causes the ensuing conflict. Wright defines the big ranchers not as simply "outside society," but representing a part of the capitalist society's dynamic, which conflicts with the communal values it proposes because of its self-interest, thus losing out to the kind of society the homesteaders strive for, which is morally favored to prevail by the Western genre (132). After he recounted his American dream and how he built his cattle empire with his own two hands at the beginning of the film, a certain compassion with the shattered Baxter towards the ending, when he falls back into a stark Irish accent, dethroned and badly bruised from the battle, is only natural: at the villain's destruction the viewer rejoices, but also feels nostalgically sorry (Cawelti 53).

As the third party in the character division, the figure of Charley embodies most traits traditionally associated with the hero. Laconic and tight-lipped throughout most of the film (cf. Cawelti 61), he exemplifies the Western's distrust of language (Tompkins 49). When Boss gets lost in his own talk of Sue and her brother, who he still thinks are husband and wife, imagining them "working on some little ones" and concluding, "Creates quite a picture, doesn't it?," Charley remarks, "Heard they're worth a thousand words," and thus bids him shut up. Most of the film follows Charley's struggle to overcome his reluctance towards women (Cawelti 61). And his traumatic Civil War past coming back on him is also an aspect he shares with many Western heroes before him (Buscombe, *Open Range*). After we hear from Charley himself that he "never had a problem with killing," we learn how his violent past made him the man he is now: the necessary explanation for his special status between savagery and society. At night, in a contemplative monologue, the camera slowly tracks out from an intimate close-up, and the cartridge belt next to his head comes into the frame as he confesses to Boss how he killed a man in his childhood, became a soldier and slaughtered civilians, and eventually came to be a gun-hand not unlike Baxter's men. While his past still determines his typically ambiguous outsider status in society, Charley has changed now in that he adheres to a paradigmatic "Code of the West," and despises the villains who violate it. When he and Boss come to pick up Mose, and Baxter threatens them with the story of how a free-grazer was killed in the town before them, Charley suggests: "Shot in the back, was he?" When they finally get to see the marred Mose, he immediately concludes that someone must have kicked their friend in the face while he was down; clearly an instant of the hero's aversion to dirty and gross forms of violence (Cawelti 60). Charley also personifies the Western hero's undercurrent reluctance and sense of loss in the face of the social progress which is necessarily favored in resolving the conflict between wilderness and civilization. When the outcome of the shootout is decided, Charley's work is done, and he is not needed anymore: the townspeople take over, they hunt down the last of Baxter's men, and things settle into place as they start to clean up the mess and restore normal town life. Charley's disturbed look and immobility reflect his powerlessness and uselessness, now that progress takes its natural course, and we might trace some disgust is his expression when he catches sight of the citizens capturing the last henchman: several against one.

Boss' character has been regarded relatively little until now, which is not entirely justified. It has been suggested above that his significance is secondary to that of the hero; nevertheless, as Charley's faithful and influential companion, he plays a crucial role. The friendship between two men, central to the plot of *Open Range*, is an archetypal Western theme (Buscombe, *Open Range*). The hero's masculine comrades traditionally function as his original social milieu until he inevitably adapts and commits himself to civilization (Cawelti 62). Cawelti writes:

> "Not only does the hero's ties of friendship motivate much of his behavior, but in most cases the great sense of honor and adherence to a highly disciplined code of behavior which sharply differentiates hero from savages and outlaws springs from his association with the masculine group." (63)

This proves true when Boss repeatedly stops Charley from executing defenseless opponents, most remarkably a young henchman towards the end of the shootout: "We came here for justice, not vengeance," he tries to convince him. But Boss' character also serves as an iconic tribute to prominent figures of mature masculinity in the history of the genre (Kitses, *Horizons West* 7). Kitses sees the introductory shot of Duvall in a proudly erect posture on horseback overlooking the wide landscape as a reference to a similar shot of Gary Cooper in Anthony Mann's *Man of the West* (1958), and a subsequent framing of Boss against the deep blue sky as "echoing Ford" (*Horizons West* 7). Associations with the John Wayne stock type have also slipped into Duvall's body language; when he leans against a pole of their makeshift outdoor shelter, the image recalls a John Wayne casually resting in the door frame in Howard Hawks' *Rio Bravo* (1958) (Fig. 9). But the parallels between John Wayne's roles and Boss are not only visually realized. As his cowboy character stands for the Westerner's code of honor, respect, tolerance and loyalty, Kitses calls him the "Fordian glue" that holds together the protagonists' relationships, "doing John Wayne duty and showing both heft and sensitivity" ("Forgiven" 26). Boss' statement at the graveside of Mose, where he refuses to talk to god ("I ain't talking to that son of a bitch"), recalls the bitterness of Wayne as Ethan Edwards in *The Searchers* (1956), declaring at the graves of the settler family that "There's no more time for praying" (Another reference to this film can be found in Charley leaving the sleeping Boss as living bait in the sheriff's office, as Ethan does with Martin in *The Searchers*). "I don't doubt your grit," Charley assures him when Boss says that he has been in some fights before the shootout, and we remember an aging, but fiercely fighting Wayne in *True Grit* (1969). As such a prototypical character, Boss' language is truly representative Western talk (apart from some more garrulous phases). The way Tompkins defines the range of the Westerner's language fits the style of Boss perfectly: pithy and dense epigrams ("We pay our way, ma'am"), sayings that bring you down ("A man's trust is a valuable thing, Button. You don't wanna lose it for a handful of cards"), minimalist language ("This ain't the way, pard"), abrupt commands, understatement, and clipping off of the indefinite article--really "antilanguage" at heart, delivering the message that language is false or ineffectual (49-51).

Fig. 9. Left: Robert Duvall as Boss Spearman in *Open Range*. Right: John Wayne in *Rio Bravo*. Still (from Cameron and Pye 85).

With this formulaic complex of characters, the narrative structure of *Open Range* automatically fits a classic Western pattern of action. Cawelti hardly elaborates on the types of situations and patterns of action in the Western, as the tripartite division of characters invariably determines the basic plot, a theme of chase and pursuit in an infinite number of variations manifested in the clash between townspeople and savages (66-7). So, the town may be attacked by the villains, and the pioneers pursue them, or the savages may capture townspeople and the hero pursues them, etc., and *Open Range* may well be read in similar terms, typically with some alternating flight and pursuit (Cawelti 67). Applying Will Wright's more rigid model of four basic Western plots (the classical plot, the vengeance variation, the transitional theme, and the professional plot) is equally possible; *Open Range* would then be categorized under the heading of the classical plot (however, incorporating a secondary theme of vengeance through the killing of Mose by the villains). Even Frank Grüber's still often quoted but now somewhat obsolete list of seven basic plots has the appropriate slot for this film, the Ranch Story (cf. Cawelti 34). This confirms the adherence of *Open Range* to the Western formula, likewise in its pattern of action, setting and context. The choices that these limiting conventions still allow are decided by Costner mostly in favor of a more sentimental outcome. When Charley rides off alone after the traditional climactic gunfight, which resolved issues with deadly finality (Buscombe, *Open Range*), the viewer might already foresee the same nostalgia and lamentation as at the departure of Shane (Cawelti 56). However, he is still riding towards the camera, and any anticipation of his final departure proves too rash. Soon he will return to Sue and confess his love to her, who now symbolizes female domesticity and settlement clearer than ever before, working among the flowers in her garden with a straw hat and the emblematic white picket fence in the background (Fig. 10). This is the perfect example for Wright's conclusion to the classical plot, where the hero surrenders his special status and is accepted by society (47).

Fig. 10. *Open Range.*

It is no surprise that Costner's film features plenty of the violence inherent not only to American film in general, but to the Western genre in particular. After Clint Eastwood's much-discussed, deconstructing approach to the issue in *Unforgiven*, Costner returns to a more carefree (and hence traditional) attitude towards Western violence and avoids this revisionist manner (Kitses, "Forgiven" 27). According to Saunders, the arguing for legitimate violence is close to the heart of the genre (24), and so the viewer is here not only supposed to draw satisfaction from the repeatedly stressed fact that Mose broke the arm of one of his offenders, and from Boss and Charley surprising and battering some of Baxter's men at their campfire, but a scene suggesting the protagonists' readiness for vigilantism is meant to inspire sympathy for them. Backed by Charley, Boss confronts Marshal Poole in the cafe and threatens to take law in their own hands, representing some of the beliefs and ideologies that triggered violent behavior in the historical West as was shown in chapter two. The idea that the people stand above the institutionalized law is reflected in

Boss' words, "Our warrant is not writ by no tin star bought and paid for! It's writ by us," and he concludes, "A man's got a right to protect his property and life." That their vigilantism is eventually idealized and morally justified mirrors the genre's tendency to appreciate and legitimize the hero taking law into his own hands. Cawelti points out the importance and symbolic function of the six-gun in the Western, not only as an equivalent to the knight's sword in the continuation of a tradition of heroism, or as a phallic symbol, but also as a mark of differentiation between the hero and the villain (59-60). So it enables the hero to engage in individual combat with objectivity and detachment, showing a controlled and aesthetic mode of killing (Cawelti 60). It will be seen that this is not entirely the case in *Open Range*. However, there is a scene which emphasizes the inseparability of the Westerners and their weapons. Before Boss and Charley ride into town, they pause for a while, only for the former to make some remarks on their individual preference of handguns. Disconnected as the scene is, it might well be read as a comment on the men's sexuality (Charley's preference of a lighter gun and the fact that he does not utter a single word in the scene suggest his suppressed longing for an ordered sexual life and his inward tenderness), but it certainly indicates the Westerners' identification with their six-guns, which are treated like fixed parts of their body and personality. On the other hand, the film presents some subtle criticisms of particular forms of violence. When his companion wants to execute one of Baxter's henchmen at their campfire, Boss stops him from doing so at the last moment, and for a moment the camera lingers on the worried look in his open face, now brightly lit by the fire and cleared of the deep furrows that usually speak of the toughening yearlong experience of the rugged Western life: beneath the surface, he is a morally pure character, who is able to differentiate between violence which is justifiable, and such which is not. This repeats itself in a later scene already mentioned above, in which Boss has to stop Charley from murdering a helpless victim again. In sum, the film makes a differentiation between "wrong" forms of violence which are condemned and legitimate forms in accordance with the Western code. When legitimate, these acts of violence are duly celebrated and aestheticized, as when Boss shoots a sniper right through the wooden boards of a shed with his shotgun: the impact flings the victim some ten feet through the air and against the wall of the neighboring house in an impressive stunt, before Boss is framed through the immense hole the charge has torn into the wall in a heroic posture (Fig. 11).

Fig. 11. *Open Range.*

So can *Open Range* be ultimately dismissed as a revisionist Western? Not in the eyes of Buscombe, who sees such qualities in the fact that *Open Range* tells a story about the ending of the West (*Open Range*), an aspect made use of in a lot of deconstructionist Westerns, as for example in *McCabe & Mrs. Miller* (1970). While it is the antagonist Baxter who tries to make clear to Boss and Charley that the free range is coming to an inevitable end at the beginning of the film ("Times change, people change, but a few holdouts never do"), Boss himself later realizes that he has in fact changed with time, and hopes to make sure that Button will not continue the cowboy lifestyle, but live in a house instead of the prairie. In his review of the film, Buscombe categorizes all three major Westerns with Costner as revisionist (*Dances With Wolves*, *Wyatt Earp*, and this film), but especially points out this latest one for its nostalgic mode (*Open Range*). However, it is not a new theme in the Western to balance nostalgia for the open range with the recognition of necessary change (Saunders 27). Kitses, on the other hand, finds a different aspect of deconstruction in *Open Range*, which is its interrogation of the taciturn Westerner ("Forgiven" 27). It has been suggested above that Charley fits the traditional definition of the laconic Western hero throughout most of the film, but Kitses has a point in noting how he is forced to become increasingly articulate in the course of the story, eventually delivering two long speeches related to his past ("Forgiven" 27). In the staging and choreography of the final gunfight, Costner deconstructs the image of orderly and foreseeable shootouts for the sake of a more authentic vision of how chaotic actual Western shootouts must have been, and according to Kitses the visualization is successful in capturing the look and feel of historical photographs of comparable events ("Forgiven" 27). After Charley prepares the viewer for this in telling Boss that "it's going to be messy like nothing you've ever seen," the many gunshots that miss, fired by protagonists and antagonists likewise, even from close range and in spite of the insufficient cover of the targets, are startling at first, but soon appreciated for their deviation from unrealistic norms of exaggerated gunfighting skills in classic Western heroes. The other uncommon trait in the hero of this film separates him further from the formulaic hero, who never uses violence until the very last moment (Cawelti 60): his urge to harm defenseless villains and thus make use of unjustifiable violence in the sense of the "Code of the West," has caused Charley to be read as a younger version of Will Munny, the protagonist in *Unforgiven* (Kitses, "Forgiven" 24). Such parallels are definitely discernible, and shots of the town during a thunderstorm clearly revoke *Unforgiven*'s Big Whiskey, while Charley flipping a glass across the bar to the head of the barman reminds of the ruthless macho behavior of countless Clint Eastwood characters. Still, the question remains whether such hints suffice to see *Open Range* as that much of a revisionist film as *Unforgiven* is generally considered to be. In fact, references to all sorts of Westerns and Western directors can be found in Costner's film; Kitses stresses parallels to the revisionist works of Sergio Leone and Sam Peckinpah, or the film *Butch Cassidy and the Sundance Kid* (1969), but also to more traditionalist directors Howard Hawks and John Ford (see above), especially to the classic *My Darling Clementine* (1946) ("Forgiven"). So the allusions to such significant works will be cautiously considered as mere tributes to milestones of the genre by Costner, which would only underline his personal attachment to the Western. After all, as Saunders suggests, a Western hero still leaves considerable room for diversity (2), and also Buscombe admits that this film is highly traditional despite its meta-discourse of the passing of the West--what makes it seem fresh and new, though, is "a host of deft little touches," details like the subplot of Sue's tea service, or the protagonists buying Swiss chocolate before the shootout (*Open Range*)

To conclude this discussion of Kevin Costner's *Open Range*, it can be said that the film adheres to the traditional Western formula in almost every aspect, and is at least an instance of a nostalgic tribute to the genre, if not an attempt to resurrect the classic form (Kitses, "Days of the Dead" 18). While other later Westerns, as for example *Pale Rider* (1985), also feature a tripartite character division, *Open Range* deviates from such revisionist approaches in that it does not mystify its hero and in telling an original story rather than a variation of an existing one (as *Pale Rider* does with *Shane*). The few deconstructive elements here are hardly sufficient to outweigh its formulaic pattern, and can partly be explained by a necessity to fulfill the expectations of a modern audience. Nevertheless, while Costner's film would probably enthuse viewers like Hembus, who generally criticizes the attempts of newer books and films to expose and wreck traditional Western myths (*Geschichte* 8), the current need for political correctness conflicts with the anti-feminist and racist tendencies of traditional forms of the genre (Weidinger, *Nationale Mythen* 154), and this leaves its mark on *Open Range*. So, the meager attempts to depict an emancipated female main character are insufficient in this respect, and the film is forced to do away with any Native Americans completely to avoid an entanglement between genre conventions and a depiction of Indians in keeping with the times (there is only one single instance in the film of Native Americans being mentioned, where they are talked about in the past tense).

3.2. *The Missing*: Women and Native Americans

Ron Howard's *The Missing* is about a middle-aged woman, Maggie (Cate Blanchett), who lives on her own remote ranch with her young daughters Lilly and Dot, and two farmhands, her semiofficial lover Brake and the Mexican Emiliano. Maggie earns a little money on the side by giving medical treatment to people in the area. One day Brake and Emiliano encounter Samuel (Tommy Lee Jones), an aged white man in Apache Indian attire who seeks medical assistance by Maggie. He turns out to be Maggie's father, against whom she holds a bitter grudge for leaving their family to live with the Apache when she was still a child. She refuses him a meal, but lets him sleep in the barn and gives him treatment the next day. She does not accept the money he tries to give her and angrily sends him away. The following day, Maggie sees Emiliano, Brake, Dot, and Lilly off to a cattle job out on the range. When they have not returned by the next morning, she takes off after them only to find Brake and Emiliano having been brutally killed by a group of Indians. Dot, who was hiding during the attack, tells her mother of the event and how the Indians took Lilly with them. Maggie rides into the next town with Dot to seek help from the sheriff, but is turned down. Back at their ranch, Samuel returns to them to offer his help in tracing the Indians and get Lilly--if possible, buy her back. They take off, and meanwhile we get to know their enemies, a group of Apache scouts who deserted the US Army, accompanied by a few whites and a photographer, who abduct girls to sell them as prostitutes to Mexico at the border. Their uncanny tyrannical leader Chidin (Eric Schweig) is a *brujo*, a witch. Maggie, Samuel, and Dot arrive at another homestead which has been raided by Chidin and his men. They encounter a cavalry there, but again Maggie is turned down when she asks them for escort. The three continue their chase and pass the last camp of their enemies, where the superstitious Samuel realizes that they are dealing with a witch. He wants to persuade Dot and Maggie to wear the Indian charms he offers them, but Maggie despises him for his impiety. Soon they come upon a Chiricahua Apache, Kayitah, and his son, members of the tribe Samuel had lived with for a while. Since the wife of Kayitah's son has also been kidnapped by Chidin's group, and as Maggie is able to treat the wounded young Indian, they decide to team up against their common enemy. However, by unlucky circumstances Chidin has come into the possession of a brush Maggie lost, and telepathically practices his witchcraft on her with the help of the hair he found in the brush. With Indian rituals and Christian prayers, the Chiricahua, Samuel, and Dot try to counteract Chidin's black magic, and Maggie gets well again. The following day, Samuel and Kayitah take off to catch up with the enemies, and leave the others behind. While Samuel offers Chidin money to buy the girls back, Kayitah attempts to free them secretly. Chidin pays no attention to Samuel's offer, but instead practices his witchcraft on the "make believe Indian." He drugs Samuel, and his men beat him up, leaving him for dead. Meanwhile, Kayitah's rescue attempt fails, because Lilly gives them away, and the Chiricahua is killed by Chidin. Despite being badly damaged, Samuel manages to find back to Maggie, Dot, and Kayitah's son. In their next attempt to free the girls they resort to a trick and take advantage of the Native American's superstition, and are finally able to free not only Lilly and the wife of Kayitah's son, but the rest of the girls as well. The coming night, anticipating the final confrontation with Chidin's group, Maggie finally reconciles with Samuel. A fierce battle evolves when the enemies attack, and eventually Samuel succeeds in killing Chidin by dragging him along down a cliff, which ends the fight but costs him his own life. In the morning, Maggie starts back with her daughters: "Let's go home," she says.

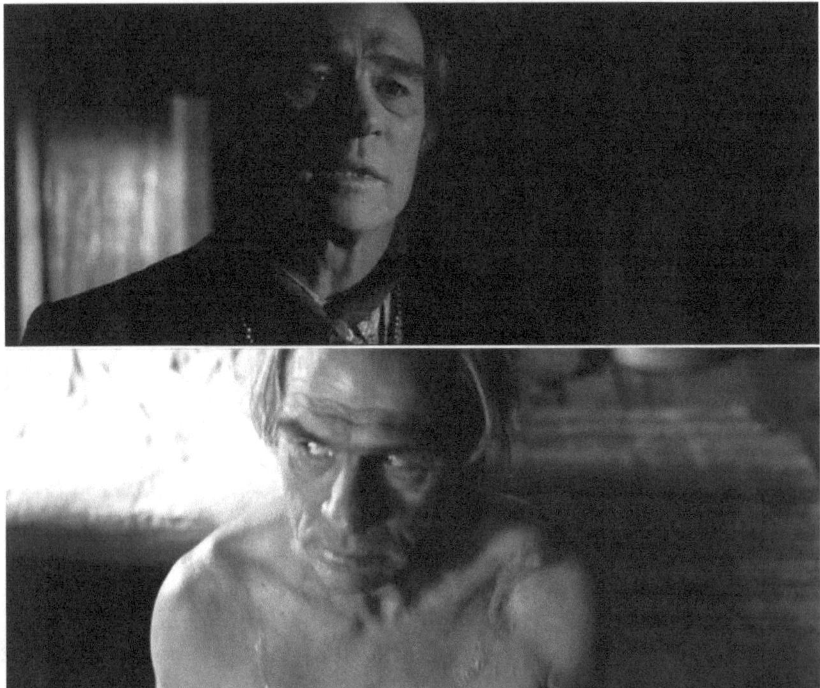

Fig. 12. *The Missing.*

After the reading of *Open Range* in terms of its relation to the classic Western above, it would only seem fair to apply a similar approach here as well. And in fact it appears that the character arrangement and narrative structure of *The Missing* may well be fitted into the genre's traditional parameters (Weidinger, *Nationale Mythen* 154). Samuel fulfills most attributes of the formulaic Western hero: as a white man who is familiar with indigenous values, he mediates between civilization and "savagery," and it is this attribute which makes him typically desirable for society to intervene in the pursuit of the villains (cf. Saunders 22). As the sheriff points out, "It takes an Apache to catch an Apache." At the same time, this attachment to Native American culture stands for the Westerners ambiguous view of civilization (cf. Cawelti 49). As an iconic anti-hero that comes riding alone in the distance near the beginning of the film, he fits the myth of the self-doubting Westerner, who has to come to terms with his past (Seeßlen and Weil 127). When he faces his past for the first time in the form of his daughter Maggie, as he steps out of the shadows into a dim light, his self-confidence has turned to shame and remorse, his sad eyes, craggy face and almost bald head depict a man who has come too late to make up for his past mistakes, and the deep scars on his taut body once he takes off his shirt speak of other wounds that have not healed (Fig. 12). Western heroes typically have an unexplainable desire to keep moving (Cawelti 64), and the same is true of Samuel, while his Apache friend Kayitah rightly realizes, "Moving spirits don't make happy men." Samuel also uses words sparingly. When Brake asks him if he has come for doctoring, it is not the only time that he does not give an (obvious) answer at all. It has been mentioned above that Wright notes a degree of friendship or respect between hero and villain (45), and since Samuel cherishes the Apache culture so much, which is not originally his, a certain tie between him and the Apache villains is suggested. The chase and pursuit narrative of *The Missing* is paradigmatic of Cawelti's suggested pattern of action (66), and finally, a climactic showdown between Samuel and Chidin (that is, hero and villain), concludes the film. However, one must not make the mistake of pigeonholing *The Missing* as a nostalgic Western concept like *Open Range*. The former consciously deviates from traditional forms in two significant aspects: the role of the female and that of the Native American. Most of the arguments in favor of the film's formulaic pattern above can be disregarded when looking at them from a viewpoint that considers the depiction of women or Native Americans. So, Samuel's attire is far from the usual Cowboy dress (Cawelti 45), and it is the female protagonist that is framed in isolation at the end, riding off at sunset (Fig. 13). Maggie herself can not be categorized in the terms of the Western's female dualism of "the blond and the brunette" (Cawelti 48).[12] While Cawelti admits a more complex relationship between hero and "savages" even in most formula Westerns, which highlights both a diabolical and noble side of the latter (52), and although *The Missing* basically does the same, this film is not as unequivocal about the role of the Native American to the narrative as usual. Here, the Indians are not simply "occasions for action" and "a problem for the hero" (Cawelti 37), but a rather more complicated issue. Director Ron Howard himself gives the clue to this balance between conventional and innovative features in *The Missing*, stating in an interview that the inspiration drawn from his experience with Westerns during his early career sometimes had to be blocked, so he could rely on the research he had done, particularly with regard to frontier women and indigenous cultures. As these two aspects seem to have produced most of the divergence from the traditional Western in *The Missing*, they shall be the focus of attention in the following.

Fig. 13. *The Missing.*

The idea to somehow correct the fixed female roles in Westerns exists at least since the fifties, when women could no longer be contented with their traditional role in the genre (Seeßlen and Weil 132; see above). [13] One result of this has already been mentioned above, *Johnny Guitar*, a film which has been much acknowledged, but also accused of a simple reversal of female roles into male ones (Seeßlen and Weil 134; see above). Evans investigates a Western with a focus of attention on women that takes a somewhat different course, *Westward the Women* (1951). This film follows a wagon trek lead entirely by women, hence centering on a whole group instead of one or two protagonists, and it stands out for its female main characters that break free of imprisoning stereotypes (Evans 206). They serve as a source of criticism of the male Westerners and their values, and force them to investigate their prejudice (Evans 206, 211). But it is eventually male initiative that liberates the female characters, who have basically transformed into honorary males (Evans 206). The women are ultimately submitted to patriarchal law, and the more energy, independence and assertiveness they mobilize in the course of the narrative, the more they seem to get punished for it through fateful events: "What the film gives with one hand [...] it takes with the other" (Evans 213).

Fig. 14. *The Missing.*

So what can *The Missing* offer to revisit the depiction of the genre's women more than fifty years later? It certainly gives a new impulse in going against the traditional female image, but notably neither by a simple inversion of a women into a gunslinger, nor by wanting to be forcibly modern or plugging itself as a "women Western" (Weidinger, *Nationale Mythen* 153-4), as other more recent films like *The Quick and the Dead* (1995), or the television series *Dr. Quinn* (1993-8) might be accused of. Like *Westward the Women*, it is a rare depiction of female courage, determination, and capacity for endurance; and neither of the two iconic Western women, the decent matron and the sexually aggressive adventuress, fit the characterization of Maggie (Evans 211). In a more far-reaching context, *The Missing* also counters films that claim historical accuracy, but still obey sex-dominated box office imperatives, which are even traceable in *Westward the Women* (Evans 211). Working independently as a healer, Maggie is irreplaceable to her community, stands up to men, and earns their respect, while her high-buttoned dresses and Blanchett's naturally beautiful, but sharp features do not force a sex-symbol image on her.

Brake never question her authority: "She's pretty firm about her hours," he assures Samuel about Maggie's terms of business, and instantly obeys when she orders him not to slam the door (mind, of her house). She does not shy away from strenuous physical labor (she is already out long in the morning chopping wood when Samuel just gets up to say his Indian prayer), and proves courage in taking up the quest for her family, or intervening in the fierce battle between Chidin and Samuel. When she has to experience men turning down her help repeatedly, she sticks to the motto she tried to drum into her daughter's head before: "Don't you ever act helpless and pitiable to win favor with a man." But when Lilly corrects her ("It's *pitiful* in English") we realize that Maggie's philosophy is not unerring. Howard claims that he made it a priority to have a female protagonist who is not just a symbol, representing encroaching civilization or one of the few other things women usually typify in Westerns, but instead a round character. So it appears that Maggie is not simply an Amazonian heroine at the other end of the scale, but a faceted human character, and not without faults. The very first shot already deconstructs any notions of a superhuman when the camera frames some old newspapers and cranes up to her daydreaming face, only to reveal in the next shot that she is involved in an only too human activity: using the bathroom (Fig. 14). Maggie has bad traits (sadistically, she tests Samuel's pain threshold when she examines him), and she has feelings. There is awkwardness about her when she sees Brake off after they spent the night together, and we assume she might be in love. At the discovery of his remains after the massacre she despairs in terror. Situations evoking unpleasant associations frame her in the foreground, facing the camera, but away from the others, so they will not see the tears she can not fight, for example, when she sees the graphophone her now missing daughter craved, or Brake's empty bed ("Come on, now," she says, telling herself she will not cry over a man--but she can not help it) (Fig. 15). It is her mysterious traumatic childhood that made her bitter and shrouds her in a repelling, isolating coldness. Often she is photographed in cold blue tones, and distanced from those around her by her position in the frame (Fig. 16). Something unspeakable haunts her and makes her talk in her sleep, and it seems to be her habit to put all the blame on her father, and her inability to forgive him that make her cold and lonely, causing her hands to shake before she doctors on him. This, however, is the flaw in *The Missing* that ultimately puts it on a similar level with a film like *Westward the Women*. Gradually, the narrative shifts its focus on Samuel, and in the course, similarly as in the latter film, Maggie gets punished for her energy, independence, and assertiveness, that is, whenever she follows her own intuition instead of Samuel's advice. By the middle of the film, she is forced to admit that she was wrong in turning him away, and not much later her emancipative behavior becomes the object of ridicule in the talk of Samuel and Kayitah. Close to the end then, her father has reestablished his authority over her: "You tell me 'yes,' or I'm not going," he urges her from on high, sitting in the saddle above her. Evans sums the end of *Westward the Women* up as follows: "a lesson has been learnt, difference reduced, identity enhanced and otherness demystified" (213), and most of this is also true for *The Missing* to a certain extent, but with the most important aspect being that the *woman* has learned a lesson on her stubbornness. The Western's inherent power balance between man and woman has been restored (admittedly it is father and daughter here, which somewhat reduces the anti-feminist aftertaste), and Samuel has duly paid his debt by sacrificing his life, leaving Maggie with a remaining guilt. Nevertheless, a foil to Maggie is provided by her daughter Lilly, who strives for femininity more in accordance with the Western stereotype and thus gets in conflict with her mother. Lilly's hedonistic ideal of beauty and coquetry is criticized as making women prey, objects, and goods in the eyes of men (Nicodemus, qtd. in Weidinger, *Nationale Mythen* 153), and that she eventually receives harsher punishment than Maggie somewhat rehabilitates the latter's ideal of emancipation.

Fig. 15. *The Missing.*

Fig. 16. *The Missing.*

One aspect in which *The Missing* undoubtedly deserves credit, though, is its attempt to portray frontier women's lives more accurately than has been done before. Even Thomson admits in his generally critical article "The Last Frontier" that this film proves how "art direction has gone some way to catching up with the real history of the West" (13). Howard admits that the story is naturally fictitious, but underlines that the makers let themselves be inspired by actual research, and this can not be denied when looking at the film attentively. The way Maggie engages in the ranch work corresponds to the image of frontier women Bartley and Loxton create, based on historical sources. Tasks nowadays mainly associated with men were necessarily also carried out by pioneer women, and an appealing montage of the day's work of Maggie, while the others are out on the range, neatly complies with an account of such in Bartley and Loxton (22-3). If Maggie's medical competence and practices seem somewhat overdrawn (she pulls an old woman's tooth, stitches the wound of Kayitah's son, and is talked about as having amputated a foot), they hardly live up to the realities, in which a single woman is said to have removed a bullet from one man, amputated several fingers of another, an stitched back the scalp of a third (25). As doctors were few on the plains, hospitals nearly non-existent, and medical supplies hard to get, the family's health was generally the responsibility of the household's woman, who would try to tackle the diseases caused by unbalanced diets and poor living conditions with folk remedies (Bartley and Loxton 24). These facts certainly add credibility to the depiction of Maggie and her character. Bartley and Loxton use similar words as Evans uses to describe the rare attributes of *Westward the Women*'s protagonists (which have turned out to fit *The Missing* as well, see above), when they try to redraw the qualities of the actual female pioneers whose accounts survived: courage, determination, and an ability to adapt (27). That the image of the independent Western female which *The Missing* presents is also not a mere flight of fancy can be seen when considering the argument that the West meant a rare opportunity for women of the late nineteenth century to break free from Victorian womanhood, which did not estimate independence as seemly: in the West they enjoyed greater freedom and often had successful careers as businesswomen (Bartley and Loxton 28-30).

The trend of "Indian sympathy" films of the nineties has clearly tapered off in more recent years, considering that hardly any of the Westerns since 2000 listed above focus on Native American characters; most of them avoid the involvement of Indians altogether, making *The Missing* the only significant exception. The reasons for this are not hard to find in a film industry still dominated by Euroamericans. Not only are movie audiences gaining in sophistication and demand more detail and authenticity in the depiction of Native Americans (Howard), but most of the relevant pro-Indian films in Western film history, even the latest ones, still receive harsh criticism by Native American scholars, for reasons often not cogent to its white producers, writers, and directors. In 1998, O'Connor claimed that "Hollywood Indians are still far from real" (38), and after an investigation of *The Missing* Thomson concludes that America is still a racist society (15). Kilpatrick finds the source for this dilemma in a cultural and communicative gap between the filmmakers and the people they depict (178). It seems that such films will always fail in realism as long as they represent stories *about* Native Americans instead of the stories Indians *tell of themselves*, even if they try to portray sympathy (Kilpatrick 178). The only solution, as Kilpatrick points out, lies in an involvement of Native Americans in powerful positions in the making of a film, to present Indians with due respect (233). All-white crews attempting to portray "Indian sympathy" in films about Native Americans will be damned if they do and damned if they do not, it seems, as accusations of euphemism, racism, or stereotyping may follow one way or the other (Kilpatrick 178). Notably, writer, producer, and director of *The Missing* are all white, and only some actors and a few consultants involved in the production are indigenous. Howard's good intentions are certainly indisputable, when he claims that it was important to him to portray the Indians in *The Missing* as characters, not merely as symbols. But when he mentions films like *A Man Called Horse* (1970) and *Little Big Man* (1970) as influential examples for a more authentic, humanistic, and detailed understanding of Native Americans, it becomes obvious on what thin ground Howard treads: these are the very films Churchill accuses of "crushing native identity under the heel of Euroamerican interpretation" in spite of their sympathetic treatment; especially *A Man Called Horse* features "hybrid" Indians, and a nonsensical mixture and simplification of tribal details and rites (700-1). These aspects, and the fact that Churchill generally condemns Westerns for establishing a very limited concept of the American indigenous people in the minds of the broad public (defined only by a short historical period and a particular geographical region) (698), make the avoidance of such issues in most recent Westerns understandable, and raise the question whether the makers of *The Missing* had better done the same. However, Shivley's investigation of the perception of Westerns among Native American and Anglo viewers gives insight into a different aspect of the matter. Shivley let equivalent groups of whites and Native Americans watch *The Searchers*, and recorded their responses to the film itself and the ethnic issues it raises. The result was that the Native Americans all responded positively, confirmed they liked it, were hardly disturbed by its (inaccurate) depiction of Indians, and declared their general appreciation of Westerns and their wish that more would still be produced (347, 351). They did actually doubt the authenticity of the portrayal, but hardly cared: in fact they mostly identified with John Wayne's character Ethan Edwards (an Indian hater in the film) (348, 351). Those asked, named *Soldier Blue* (1970), a typical early "Indian sympathy" film condemning an Indian massacre by the US Army, as a bad Western (Shivley suspects because such films evoke unpleasant emotions), and gave the depiction of the cowboy's way of life and the magnificent settings of *The Searchers* as reasons why they liked this one (Shivley 351, 353). From this point of view, and since the Native American viewers seemed to value humor in a Western, and toughness and bravery in its hero (the Anglos had divergent priorities here) (Shivley 353, 354), it may be suspected that *The Missing* would enjoy similar appeal among an indigenous audience.[14] Nevertheless, Shivley emphasizes the relative low education level among the test group, and adds that a test run of the project among an audience of Native American college students showed quite different results; here the viewers were bothered by the stereotypes and inaccuracies of the presentation (356). Interestingly, they admitted to be generally fond of Westerns as well, but preferred pure cowboy-versus-cowboy-conflicts (an example for this would obviously be *Open Range*), or Indian-versus-Indian-conflicts (one could cautiously argue that this is the case in *The Missing*) (357). Conflicting views between a broader uneducated mass of Native Americans and more educated ones certainly create a significant ethical dilemma, and providing a solution to the problem will not be attempted here. It shall only be stressed, as by Shivley, that education obviously increases the awareness of incongruous anti-Indian biases in Angloamerican culture (357).

The Missing employs some tactics to present an appropriate picture of Native Americans in keeping with the times, and to circumvent the most common critiques that such portrayals in Westerns usually have to face. However, for reasons suggested above, not all of these are perfectly successful. When Ron Howard makes claims of historical accuracy in the film's details, this is hard to prove, but he may be given the benefit of the doubt. The actors apparently took great pains to acquire an authentic Apache dialect (Howard), and Bartley and Loxton suggest that abductions of white women by Indians have indeed occurred during the white settlement of the West (45). The film then makes both Indians on the protagonist and antagonist side Apaches, trying to avoid the fatal cliché of downright good and bad Native American tribes, as was for example criticized in *Dances With Wolves* (1990) (see above). A symbolic chase of Indians by Indians with the white protagonists standing by and watching, comments on formulaic chases between cowboys and Indians in traditional Westerns. By featuring some biased characters with ludicrous prejudices against Native Americans, *The Missing* simultaneously exposes these, such as when Lilly tells her younger sister that Indians are "gut-eaters," or when Maggie explains how her father "turned Indian" some time ago: "turn your back, he'll eat your dogs and horses." When she has to treat Kayitah's son, and not only suspects Indians carry diseases, but expresses unease since she has never treated one, Samuel counters with a sarcastic remark to suggest human equality. One aspect in later films about Native Americans which has been positively acclaimed in contrast to traditional depictions is a portrayal of their natural sense of humor, as in *The Outlaw Josey Wales* (1976) or *Dances With Wolves*. Since Shivley's field study suggests that especially Native American audiences value humor, this emphasis on humanness seems to be a sensible tactic, which also *The Missing* makes use of. Kayitah and Samuel repeatedly crack insider jokes about their wives or about the cultural differences between Indians and whites, and the name the Chiricahua have given Samuel is the object of laughs several times, as it translates into English with "shit-for-luck." Technically, Samuel is of course no Native American, but he represents respect and appreciation for the Apache culture in the film, so it is notable that he seems to take his own ritualistic Indian prayer not too seriously: he ends it quite abruptly and unimpressed, turning to the fascinated Dot with the laconic remark, "If you got something to say, say it." Even the evil Chidin and his men show a sense of humor (but a vicious one, as may be guessed), when they lampoon the photographer who accompanies them. Next, *The Missing* features some critical comments that highlight its awareness of the intricate ethnic conflict, not only in frontier history, but also in the Western genre. Although Samuel is basically the hero, there is an implicate criticism of his attempt to copy the ways of a culture that is not his, when Chidin calls him a "make believe Indian," humiliates him and threateningly predicts that he was born white but will die an Indian (but sooner than Samuel may wish). In the same way, an encounter of Samuel with an Apache scout of the US Army and their verbal confrontation provides ground for reflection on the ethical issues of cultural contact. However, Walters disapproves of this forceful jumble of cultures and interrogation of morals:

"*The Missing* takes pains to distribute credit and blame across its ethnic divide: the marauders include whites and the girl's rescue would be impossible without Samuel's Chiricahua chums. This confusion extends to an institutional level: the offenders are in fact deserters from an army that loots their victim's homes [...]. It's hard, though, to discern the implications of such ambiguities [...]. Here the options are simply good and evil."

When one army officer says, "This whole territory is topsy-turvy: Indians running with whites, whites running with Indians," he sums up what the filmmakers must have seen as the only way to avoid a good-culture-versus-bad-culture structure. This continues in a curious questioning and juxtaposition of contrasting religious values between Native Americans and whites throughout the film, eventually involving supernatural elements. Opposite Maggie's Christianity, her prayers, and the crucifix she wears around her neck, stand Samuel's adherence to the Chiricahua religion, his seemingly superstitious beliefs, and the Indian charms he wears and eventually distributes among his family. The obvious message is that neither religion is better or worse: after Maggie has been acclaimed a good Christian by Brake, we see her hiding the necklace before she proposes fornication. She says a Christian prayer in order to fatally hit her rifle's aim, and eventually it is her necklace that gives away Kayitah when he tries to rescue his son's wife and Lilly. On the other side, Samuel says his prayers mainly because he hopes for a cure of his rattlesnake bite, distresses his family with his mythical stories, and gives an Indian charm to Dot of which we never know whether it made her almost drown, or really saved her from drowning. But ultimately it is the amalgamation of both religions that saves the protagonists from harm: when Maggie falls sick by Chidin's magic, seemingly equally shallow "Indian chants compete with Old Testament readings for remedial effect" (Walters), and it is not clear whether it is the emblematic hawk Samuel calls for help, or Maggie's prayer that leads his way back to her after he has been drugged by Chidin.

Notwithstanding these efforts, some problems in *The Missing*'s depiction of Native Americans remain. Besides some more or less stereotypical features in some Indian characters--their inability to speak English on the negative side, and the metaphorical braveness of Kayitah and his son on the positive side,--the most "Indian" character the viewer really gets to know well is white: Samuel. This allows for the involvement of some Indian stereotypes which would prove fatal in a depiction of "real" Native Americans in a present-day Western. He bears it without the utterance of a single word when Maggie test his pain barrier (see above), he has the ability to read traces exaggeratedly well, and the extent to which he portrays his belief in Indian rites and myths mounts into the absurd, and is thus ridiculed. The point of the fable he tells Maggie when she asks for his reasons to go live with the Native Americans is opaque, so the film never explains the motivation for making the hero a white man with Indian skills, and we never quite know why Samuel became an Apache (Thomson 13). This is essential, as it makes the film liable to heavy reproaches: Churchill criticizes that Westerns exclusively define indigenous people in terms of their interaction with whites, and demonstrate the superiority of Euroamerican minds (698, 702). Both is true of *The Missing*; note that Samuel outlives Kayitah and outwits Chidin, the two most prominent Native Americans in the film.

To sum up this analysis of *The Missing*, it has been shown that the film makes some attempts to come to terms with two major defects in the formula Western, by deconstructing traditional images of women and Native Americans. It is successful in making Maggie an undoubtedly feminine heroine, prominently set apart from typical female figures in Westerns in a positive sense; but it can not transcend certain limits the Western mythology imposes on the portrayal of gender (Weidinger, *Nationale Mythen* 154). The presentation of Native Americans is more problematic, and here *The Missing* employs some significant tactics, mainly to avoid a siding with either Euroamerican or indigenous cultures. However, the proclaimed burden of the mainstream film industry to clear away misunderstandings, derision, hatred, and nostalgic guilt that have defined the American Indian on screen, weighs a little too heavy on this film (Kilpatrick 233), and it can not entirely break away from some Anglocentric biases. Opposite this revisionist side stands nostalgia for the traditional Western which surfaces in a basically formulaic character and action pattern, and obvious parallels to classic Westerns. These have not been duly mentioned here yet for reasons of space, but the analogies to films like *The Searchers*, *Ulzana's Raid* (1972), or *Shane* can hardly be overlooked. Especially the character of Dot provides a curious equivalent to *Shane*'s Joey. Like Shane's gunfighter past to Joey, Samuel's Indian past is a fascinating mystery to Dot, whose playful appliance of "war paint" goes together with Joey's play with his wooden revolver. If the gunfighter's violence provides the necessary, but soon obsolete vehicle for the white pioneering of the West in *Shane*, where Joey symbolizes the future of America (cf. Hembus, *Lexikon* 432), it seems to be the Indian way of life that has to tragically sacrifice itself in *The Missing* to live on nostalgically in Dot, the country's (white) hope for the future (note the stars-and-stripes pattern of her jacket (Fig. 17)).

Fig. 17. *The Missing.*

3.3. *3:10 to Yuma*: Remake of a Classic

3:10 to Yuma, directed by James Mangold, centers around Civil War veteran Dan Evans (Christian Bale), now a luckless small-time rancher living with his wife Alice and his two sons Will and Mark on a small homestead. A continuing drought and heavy debt endanger his business, as henchmen of the creditor Hollander put fire to their barn one night. Dan stops his assertive son Will from firing at them, and decides to negotiate about credit one more time the next day. On their way, Dan and his sons witness how the gang of notorious outlaw Bend Wade (Russell Crowe) holds up a stagecoach in a fierce and bloody battle that costs several lives, and in the course of events requires the leader Wade to shoot a member of the money transport escort, as well as one of his own gang. When the gang spots Dan and his sons, the rancher demands back his cattle, which have been used by Wade to hold up the wagon. Wade, however, takes their horses so they will not follow him, but grants him they will get everything back. The outlaws then ride into the near town, Bisbee, where they hide their identity and trick the marshal and deputies, and the railroader Butterfield, in anticipation of the stagecoach, into leaving the town to find the very highwaymen that have supposedly held up the transport, to get rid of them. The gang has a drink in a saloon, where Wade recognizes the barmaid as an old romance and dance hall singer he used to know. When they are alone, he begins to flirt with her, and eventually they have sex. In the meantime, Dan and his sons have found a surviving, but wounded Pinkerton detective of the escort. They start dragging him away until they come upon their horses, which Wade has left them as promised. Soon they encounter the party of Butterfield and the marshal with his deputies, who realize they have been deceived. Dan sends his sons home and heads to Bisbee with the rest, where he tries to negotiate with Hollander, while the local doctor, Potter, removes a bullet from Byron, the surviving detective. In his final despair, Dan offers Hollander a brooch belonging to his wife as a payment, but the creditor refuses. In the saloon Dan encounters Wade, whose men have already left town, and not only manages to sponge a few dollars from the tranquil outlaw as a retaliation, but so also distracts him long enough until the marshal and his men can arrest him. A team is rounded up to escort Wade to Contention, where he is to be put on the 3:10 train to Yuma prison, including Butterfield, Doc Potter, Hollander's henchman Tucker, and Byron. They need one more man, so Dan seizes the opportunity to offer his help in exchange for 200 dollars, and Butterfield agrees. The team and the prisoner have dinner at Dan's ranch, where Wade flirts with Dan's wife and leaves an impression on his sons. When they set off for Contention, Dan refuses his son Will's plea to accompany them. However, Will follows them secretly, and things start happening fast on the way to Contention. Wade kills first Tucker and then Byron, almost coming into power over his captors until Will steps in and forces him to surrender. When they take a shortcut through Apache territory, they survive an Indian attack only through the adventurous skill of Wade, who uses his momentary dominance to get away from Dan and the rest. He turns up in a railroad camp, where a posse recognizes the wanted outlaw and seizes and tortures him. Butterfield's escort coming after him demands their captive back. Things escalate; Doc Potter is shot and dies. But Butterfield, Dan, Will, and Wade get away and are on their way to Contention again to arrive there soon. Meanwhile, Wade's gang, now led by his unscrupulous right-hand man Charlie Prince, have found out that their boss is being escorted to Contention to be put on the 3:10 to Yuma, and catch up. In Contention, Wade is brought to a hotel room to be watched by Dan there until the train arrives. Playfully, the outlaw tries to bribe Dan with 1.000 dollars (to buy himself and his wife "everything she ever wanted"), but although he visibly contemplates, Dan does not make any comment. Not long thereafter, Charlie Prince and the rest of Wade's gang arrive, and aggravate Dan's situation by offering money to the townspeople if they kill one of Wade's captors. As a result, one after the other on Dan and Butterfield's side drop out, and eventually Butterfield himself, who assures Dan that he has done his duty and may let Wade go; he would even be paid the promised sum. Still, and although even Will does not expect any more heroism of his father, Dan refuses to give in. He lets Butterfield promise to bring Will home safely and pay his wife 1.000 dollars. Eventually, he drags Wade out and towards the station under the hail of bullets of the outlaw's gang. Dan is shot, the train is late, and they barricade in the station building. Charlie Prince, who keeps coming after them, is stopped by Will, who has decided not to abandon his father, and lets a fenced in cattle herd trample over Wade's companion. The train arrives and Wade gets on it, when Dan is suddenly shot in the back by Charlie, who has survived the cattle stampede. Wade's gang gathers around him and returns his gun belt to him. After a moment of contemplation, the outlaw quickly shoots all remaining members of his gang dead, including Charlie. Will approaches to see for his father, who is evidently dying. He assures Dan that he has accomplished his mission and aims his gun at Wade. A few moments pass with the two in opposition, until Will lowers his gun. Wade gets on the train voluntarily, and as the train sets off, a short whistle lets his horse gallop after the "3:10 to Yuma."

This film earns its prominent position in this paper for at least one simple reason: as a relatively faithful remake of one celebrated Western classic, *3:10 to Yuma* (1956), the changes that have been made from the original, next to those features that stayed the same, may vividly reveal what characterizes an "up-to-date" Western in relation to a "classic." As has been seen above, it is not the only recent remake of a classic Western; but its fellow combatant, *The Alamo*, did not enjoy nearly as much success and critical acclaim, neither in its original of 1960, nor in its remake of 2004. This said, it is in a way wrong to stamp off the original *3:10 to Yuma* as a "classic" Western so thoughtlessly. Directed by Delmer Daves, one of America's most forgotten directors and a successful innovator of the Western genre during the fifties (Tevernier 42; Hanisch 279), *3:10 to Yuma* (1956) was a film much ahead of its time. Not only did the combination of a ruthless killer and a sexually attractive lover in Wade's character (Glenn Ford), and the suggestive seduction scene between him and Emmy break censorship taboos of the time (Walker 143; Tavernier 48), but by contrasting a brutal outlaw at the settler family's table with the glamorous gunfighter of *Shane*, the film already pointed "the way towards the development of the Western hero in the sixties and beyond" (Walker 143). But the most striking aspect of *3:10 to Yuma* (1956) is the character of Dan Evans (Van Heflin). As he becomes a hero involuntarily, out of economic necessity, and to regain his wife's respect, Seeßlen and Weil see in him the most impressively "de-heroized hero" (142; see above). To enhance the contrast to conventional Western heroes, Dan does not become a hero for good, in spite of his heroic deed, but returns contentedly to his work-laden and unglamorous life (Seeßlen and Weil 142). Other than *High Noon*'s Will Kane, Dan Evans does not act out of a sense of responsibility determined by maxims of the Westerner's life, but is motivated by a need for survival and the wish not to fail for once in his life (Hanisch 280). It would of course be possible to analyze James Mangold's remake of *3:10 to Yuma* as an individual contemporary representative of the genre, but for the significance and originality of its model, and in order to discern telling differences between two closely related Westerns of distinct eras, the main focus of attention shall be a comparison of remake and original here. An investigation of variations in plot structure, characterization, the aspect of heroism, and the predominant ideology will prove most fruitful, but also the visualization of the two films shall be contrasted, and issues of gender and ethnicity in the 2007 film will shortly be mentioned.

The basic story line and character complex of the remake differ from the original in several ways. A number of scenes were added or varied (increasing the running time of the original 92 minutes to 122), characters where added or given more emphasis, others were deleted or significantly changed, and the ending is essentially different. The main figures are a little to greatly differently characterized. Hardly a scene was deleted or shortened, except for the act with Dan and Wade in the hotel room, the heart-piece of the original, which is less than half as long in the remake. The major scenes in Mangold's film, which are not to be found in that of 1956 are the opening with Dan's burning barn until the holdup of the stagecoach (which again is much extended, like the rest of the action scenes, including loads of additional stunts and violence), the entire sequence of Wade's transportation from Dan's ranch to Contention and all the happenings on the way, the aspect that Charlie Prince offers the townspeople of Contention money if they kill Wade's captors, and the tragic ending: the original film ends with Dan getting successfully and unharmed on the train with Wade, riding off to wave to his family in the distance while it starts to rain. In the 1956 film are no such characters as the Pinkerton detective Byron and the henchman Tucker, and the remake's Doc Potter seems to be meant as only a remote equivalent to the original's Alex Potter, a town drunk who volunteers to stick with Dan through the end, but is brutally killed by the gang and hanged in the hotel lobby as a warning. This killing of Alex Potter crucially adds to Dan's moral motivation to see the job through, an element that is missing in the remake. The character of Charlie Prince is much less emphasized in the original, just like Dan's son Will, who does not follow the party to Contention there, and is naturally not involved in the finale either. Dan Evans appears more pitiable and vulnerable in the remake, and Wade is a slightly darker character here, and more vehement and ambivalent than in Daves' version. The question that remains is why these changes where made. One could argue that some scenes and characters, like the transportation scene (in which the additional characters of Tucker and Byron are killed anyways), were mainly included to increase the running time, which has obviously risen on the average since the fifties, especially in supposedly sophisticated films. The argument that the remarkably greater extent of violence and action where mainly added to appeal to younger audiences is plausible, and this could also explain the shortening of the hotel room sequence, which adds to the general pace of the new version. On the other hand, some of the added and varied scenes help to point out changes in the characterization, which, in turn, mark an utterly new and more ambiguous view on the aspects of ideology, morality, and heroism of the original in its remake, as shall be illustrated in the following.

Both in the original of 1956 and the remake of 2007, Dan's character is a hero that does not at all conform to the Western formula; he is actually part of the townspeople character group, the society, and in the end of the original story he reintegrates into it. So what has been said of Van Heflin's character in the 1956 film, that he has none of the features of the traditional Western hero and is rather pitiful than heroic (Hanisch 280), applies to the remake as well. However, Mangold's film somewhat overdraws these aspects. In the original Dan is characterized as the "leave-me-alone" type of person, who keeps out of trouble because it is not his business: "I work alone," he assures Wade at one point. When asked to escort Wade to Contention, he says he is no deputy and it is not his job, and this egoism and lack of a sense of community is the fault he has to overcome in the original film. In the remake, it is much more Dan's lack of bravery that troubles him. He keeps out of trouble as well, but we get the feeling that he would like to cause trouble if he only dared. What Tavernier calls a reluctance to violence in Heflin's character (47), has turned into a repression of violence in Christian Bale's: three times Dan is on the verge of firing his rifle in the 2007 film, but retreats in the last moment, uncocks the weapon, and so puts his tail between his legs. When he is then forced to give one of his cattle the *coup de grâce*, it is a gratification to him that he may fire without impediment. Casting Christian Bale as Dan Evans, the remake underlines significant differences to the original.

Van Heflin's performance is more or less a reprise of his role as Joe Starrett in *Shane*, and audiences of the time must have been used to him as such: a plain, hard-working everyman, sort of bulky, and not without a physical powerfulness. Bale is usually not typecast in any such way, but, on the contrary, known for accepting a great diversity of roles that come with a changing physicality, ranging from a half-starved, subjugated social outcast in *The Machinist* (2004) to an athletic, superhuman action hero in *Batman Begins* (2005). His portrayal of Dan Evans in *3:10 to Yuma* (2007) tends towards the former, making him a much more fragile and subordinate character than in the original. Bale's slim face and hollow eyes contrast with Heflin's embittered, but resolute, granite-hewn countenance. When Dan and Wade wrestle toward the ending of the remake (a scene which is absent in the original as well), Wade quickly gains the upper hand. This is something we could hardly imagine of Glenn Ford's Wade in a confrontation with Heflin's Dan, whose exercise from the hard physical labor on the ranch would probably have given him greater strength than a happy-go-lucky gunman, as is also suggested in *Shane*. Of course there is a certain clumsiness in Heflin's brute force; so he gives away their hotel room hideout when he knocks down an intruder trying to lynch Wade, and a gunshot goes off, but the scene indicates a physical strength in Dan which is not emphasized in the remake. In the 2007 film, Dan lacks any authority: he lets himself be screamed at by Byron and is humiliated and pushed around by Tucker, so that he goes down to the floor and literally has to beg Hollander for credit in exchange of his wife's brooch on his knees--an image, which recalls Dan telling his wife in the 1956 film: "I hate to beg people for help." While nobody pays attention to Dan's pitiful attempts to give orders in the remake (he commands Wade to go to sleep and tells Will not to listen to him equally unsuccessfully), it is the enervated Dan in the original who shouts at people and confidently tells Wade, "Well if you're quiet like me, then shut up like me." If Heflin's Dan is a born loser and coward in the eyes of his wife and sons, as Hanisch describes him (279), Bale's Dan personifies a clear enhancement of these qualities.

Also in the character of Ben Wade Mangold's remake shows some subtle, but relevant differences to the original. The Wade of the 1956 *3:10 to Yuma* has always been noted for his ambiguity, being both violent and lovable, leaving no doubt about his qualities and superiority over Dan in intelligence, fantasy, sensitivity, wit, and composure (Hanisch 280; Hembus, *Lexikon* 750). Thus, despite constant reminders that he has ruthlessly killed two people in the beginning, the viewer starts to sympathize with

Wade. Also the remake goes to great lengths to underline Wade's appreciable qualities, depicting him as a romantic and dignified icon. Elegantly costumed, he sits in the saddle in a knightly, aristocratic manner; we learn that he is a literary ("Have you ever read another book than the Bible?" he questions Byron) and artistic man, calmly drawing sketches of impressions even in precarious situations. He appears to adhere to some sort of "Code of the West" and refrains from killing the defenseless surviving Pinkerton detective (Charlie's colt in the foreground reminds us that *he* would certainly not hesitate to do so). However, Wade's darker, violent side is shown in such a way that it notably stresses his ambivalent character. He brutally slaughters Tucker with a fork, and keeps hitting him in a fit of rage, when the other is long overpowered, and it is a similar uncontrollable impulsiveness that makes him throw Byron down over a cliff. Recalling Delmer Daves' film, in which Glenn Ford's Wade sounds convincing when he assures Dan he likes to do things "real peacefully," and tries to twist the events to make it sound like him killing the two men was self-defense (which, of course, sounds not that convincing--but the disposition is what counts here), it is hard to imagine this character committing the deeds that Russell Crowe's Wade does. While Dan's son Will might certainly not be utterly wrong when he tells Wade of his conviction that he "ain't all bad," the outlaw denies it nevertheless. However, the fact that he still tries to save Dan's life in the final shootout, and those of his captors in the Apache attack (which he also denies later on), and that we learn of his childhood experiences which might provide an explanation for his fateful choice of career, further support his enigmatic characterization. This manifests itself as well in his sense of irony, which is constantly displayed, especially in his attitude towards religion, which makes him a less jovial character than in the original. Several times, Mangold's film emphasizes the handle of Wade's shiny gun, embroidered with a brass crucifix. "Careful, the gun's got a curse on it," he remarks cynically when a deputy takes it away from him at his arrest, well aware of the paradoxical ornamentation. The detail is again stressed in the climactic scene when Wade shoots all remaining members of his gang in one go, after the assassination of Dan, where it mirrors the overall ambivalence of the ending, which leaves open whether Wade is now a converted, or the bad guy *par excellence*, killing all his companions to get away with the haul on his own (Heller, E-mail). Wade's opaque attitude towards Christianity is further displayed in the scene where he questions the piousness of Byron, who was involved in an Apache massacre slaughtering women and children ("Apparently he thought Jesus didn't mind. Jesus don't like the Apache," he provokes him), and his frequent use of Bible quotations to support rather "impious" thoughts and arguments. So he quotes the Bible before he justifies the killing of his own gang member, or before he tries to flirt with Alice, Dan's wife. This, by the way, brings us to the more intruding manner of Wade in the remake, in opposition to the original. In Daves' film of 1956, it seems to take Wade a little less effort to seduce women. In the 2007 version it is him who starts asking Alice at the dinner table somewhat out of the blue if she does not happen to come from San Francisco, whereas in the original he weaves this ploy into the conversation much more elegantly.

Fig. 18. *3:10 to Yuma* (2007).

With these slightly altered depictions of the main characters comes a reworked view of the Western heroism the story focuses on so much. In fact, two key scenes that determine the outcome of the original film are missing in the remake. The character of Alex Potter is basically absent here (see above), and so is the conflict that arises out of him being lynched by Wade's gang. Because in the 1956 film, following this event, Alex Potter's brother breaks into the hotel room to kill Wade as retaliation. That Dan stops him from doing so ultimately motivates Wade to cooperate when he is being dragged into the train: "I don't like owing anybody any favors. You saved my life back at the hotel," Wade tells Dan. Walker points out that Dan goes through with the act of putting Wade on the train, not because of the money (which Butterfield offers to pay him anyways), but for the murdered Alex Potter, which eventually turns his task into an act of selfless heroism (145). The absence of this significant detail is made up for by a different aspect in Mangold's remake. Here, Dan's Civil War past is stressed, which has left a mark on his body by his amputated leg. But not until near the very end of the film we learn that it has also left a mark on his soul: he has lost his leg by embarrassing circumstances, not by any heroic deed, and since then has to live with the thought in the back of his mind that his younger son Mark wrongly thinks his father a war hero (and not until that scene do we realize the hidden shame we saw in Dan's smile at Mark when he boasted with his father's heroism at the dinner table (Fig. 18)). This is something Dan has decided he can not live with, and it is what drives him to complete his task despite the odds that are constantly against him--as Macnab notices, his heroism lies in his refusal to accept his plight. However, the remake makes it much more improbable from the beginning that Dan will survive the walk to the station. Charlie Prince in himself is depicted as a much fiercer threat, and he also turns the townspeople of Contention against the rancher. Facing the unlikeliness of his survival, Dan at one point realizes that he might not make it, but he is willing to sacrifice his life to gain the status of a hero and the deserved respect of his sons and wife. He makes sure the future and wealth of his family are taken care of, and tells Will to "remember: it was your old man walked Ben Wade to the station when nobody else wanted." As "the man who walked Ben Wade to the station," he is tempt to become a legend of the West, and Wade's sketch of Dan as he sits by the window with the shotgun on his lap and awaiting his fate foreshadows this mythical image (Fig. 19). This is a pivotal contrast to the concept of the original film, where Dan's heroism is not in danger of becoming the essential meaning of his life, and where he does not turn into living legend, and neither into a hero who is nothing else besides just that (Hembus, *Lexikon* 750; Seeßlen and Weil 142).

Fig.19. *3:10 to Yuma* (2007).

There is, however, another way to read Dan's motivation to see his job through in the 2007 *3:10 to Yuma*, which connects to his relationship with his son Will. While the motif of the son doubting his father's manliness is also present in the original film, it receives much greater attention here, with Will's character being involved in most of the action until the very end (cf. Weidinger, "Re: Nationale Mythen"). The film constantly stresses Will's growing admiration and idolatry for the outlaw Ben Wade, opposed to a loss of respect for his father. In the beginning it is shown that he is a lover of dime novels; when Dan stops him from shooting at the outlaws, saying that he will take care of it, this is doubted by Will who later assures him, "I ain't never walking in your shoes." "He's fast," is all Will manages to stammer when he sees Wade shoot, and adoration is in his eyes when he listens to Wade's talk of the outlaw lifestyle at the campfire. Not even Dan's instant reminder that the taking of innocent lives comes with such a way of life can diminish Will's worship of the gunman, and when Wade knocks out the father in front of his son's eyes not much later, this will certainly not help Dan to reestablish his authority. So it affords more drastic measures of Dan, not only to regain his son's respect, but to convince him that the violence and destruction of families that accompanies the life of an outlaw in no desirable prospect. Eventually he sacrifices his life for the cause, but whether he succeeds remains as blurred in the end as the overall moral. Wade hands over his gun belt to Will: is this the rancher son's initiation into the life of a gunfighter, or is Wade setting a positive example by giving up his outlaw lifestyle? Weidinger might support the latter view, as he sees the function of the greater emphasis on Will's character mainly in providing a fairly happy ending with a sort of positive outlook into the future ("Re: Nationale Mythen"). On the other hand, Wade's horse running after the train would rather support the possibility that he will escape from the "3:10 to Yuma" to collect his gang's loot for himself, as Heller suggests (E-mail; see above). The fact is that Wade's character remains equivocal; the final expression on his face might be one of guilt and remorse, or one of coldness and determination with equal likability (Fig. 20). Since Macnab points out that the lines between good and evil are constantly blurred in *3:10 to Yuma* (2007), it may be assumed that Wade is not the simple antagonist opposition to Dan, as their formulaic contrasting bright and dark hats and costumes would ironically suggest.

Fig. 20. *3:10 to Yuma* (2007).

A bias which seems fairly visible in the recent *3:10 to Yuma*, though, and which makes it stand out from the original as well, is an ideological emphasis on money and materialist values. The 1956 film generally puts more stress on Wade's disruption of the transport than on his theft of gold, which is not seen at all and hardly mentioned or talked about, whereas in the remake the opening of the money box by the bandits and its contents are deliberately shown to heighten the viewer's awareness that money was stolen. The essential alteration of the original dialogue, however, is Wade's answer to Dan's modest claim, "I make an honest living" in the remake, upon which the outlaw responds, "It might be honest, but it ain't much of a living." This statement seems to stick in the rancher's mind, and ultimately causes him to demand of Butterfield that he provides his wife and family with the 1.000 dollars Wade originally tried to bribe him with. This detail is obviously supposed to give modern viewers the satisfaction that Dan's family will eventually become as wealthy as they deserve, and might even give up the ranching lifestyle (as Wade suggested, the sum would be sufficient to do so), a supposedly "happy ending" in spite of Dan's death. This is a most sharp contrast to the ideology the original film conveys, where Dan and Alice are portrayed as "a truly adult couple, bruised by the rigors of life, but enduring" (Tavernier 49). In Daves' film, the more traditional Western creed that individual pioneering needs to prevail in the face of Eastern incorporation is predominant. Alice seems to be complaining about their arduous life at first, but finally confesses to Dan, "I love everything, every minute, all the worry, and the work" (cf. Walker 145). This key line of dialogue is missing in the remake as well, and while the arrival of rain in the original finally resolves all conflicts and guarantees the happy continuation of the pioneer life of the Evans family, no rain is needed in the remake: sudden material wealth, a metaphor for the American dream, seems to make up for all losses. On this basis, one might cautiously presume that materialistic values play an even greater role in the America of today.

Fig. 21. *3:10 to Yuma* (2007).

One aspect of recent Westerns which has hardly received any attention here yet is their visual style. Basically, the films discussed so far adhere to the presently predominant principles of mainstream Hollywood film-making, as most Westerns of the fifties, for example, conformed to the fashion of their time (Saunders 14). Nevertheless, as the case of *3:10 to Yuma* allows a direct comparison between two more or less equivalent films of two eras 50 years apart, their different visualization and style of direction shall shortly be looked at here. Delmer Daves' film has been praised for the quality of its black-and-white photography, which he chose instead of color to create a feeling of dryness (Hembus, *Lexikon* 750). His refusal to soften contrasts with filters, using the hard switches from light to shadow to create an atmosphere of threat (Hembus, *Lexikon* 750), resulted in a style which Tavernier calls paradoxical: at once realistic and theatrical (49). All these features are naturally absent in the remake, which was chosen to be made in color (not surprisingly, considering the current unpopularity of black-and-white film), but Macnab is basically right when he points out that Mangold avoids deliberate anachronisms or elaborate framing devices to maintain a relatively traditional style. However, the strong influence of the Italian Western is hardly discernible in the visualization of 2007's *3:10 to Yuma* (see above). The introductory shot of Wade, whose face is only revealed when the brim of his hat tilts upwards (Fig. 21), or the medium to extreme close-ups in which Charlie Prince (a typical cold-blooded, immoral, and cynical Italowestern bad guy) is frequently framed, point in that direction, as does the depiction of the grotesquely explicit violence: Wade kills two men by shooting them in the neck, and gruesomely slaughters Tucker by slitting his throat with a fork, and the removal of the bullet from Byron's stomach is vividly portrayed.[15] While Tavernier claims that the action scenes and movements of violence in Delmer Daves' films are swift, even lightening fast, and taking Wade's cold-blooded murder of the stagecoach driver as an example for the director's knowledge of how to film violence, he stresses that Daves "pays more attention to what brought the violence about, or to its results" (47-8). Mangold, on the other hand, seems to put great effort in making up for this supposed lack of focus on action scenes and violence in the original. Where only a handful of characters die in the 1956 film and most of these deaths each cause a crucial turn in the plot, the remake slaughters an army of Pinkerton detectives, kills civilians in overcrowded towns, and introduces several new characters whose fate is always a violent death. Such aspects, and the dramatization of most of the other action scenes, cause a disparity between original and remake which can hardly be compensated for by Mangold's few obvious visual references to the 1956 film, like the coachman's point of view and focus on the horses' shadows in one of the stagecoach rides, the shot of the collapsed coach on the little bridge in front of Dan's ranch (Fig. 22), or the general resemblance of the Evans farmhouses of both films, and the actresses playing Emmy (or Emma, as she is called in the 2007 film). As a consequence, the 2007 film has been criticized as an "overblown and overextended remake" of a film marked for its relative humility: "Almost everything about it [Daves' version] is quiet [...], the film is almost the antithesis of the typical shoot-'em-up Western, preferring to concentrate on parched landscapes and equally parched family life" (Last, "A Quiet American"). Tavernier further accentuates the composure of Daves' cinema by suggesting that only "images of peace and quiet" could summarize his cinema in one scene, a definition that hardly fits Mangold's fast-paced style of direction in the remake (48). One could take the comparison further by juxtaposing the musical score of the films, with the 1956 film's elegiac theme melody (which becomes diegetic and self-reflective when Wade whistles the tune) contrasting heavily with the pompous, rhythmic soundtrack of the remake. But the essential question that remains is why these changes were undertaken. As *3:10 to Yuma* (2007) still shows relative faithfulness to the original in comparison to similar reprisals of classic Westerns or Western plots, it shall be suggested here that in spite of the many alterations, the remake does not seem to be motivated first and foremost by a deconstruction of its model. Instead, it must be considered that in a large-scale production like Mangold's film, contemplations of economy, and hence the necessary appeal to a young audience might easily outweigh artistic ambitions or the faithfulness to an accomplished classic. Older audiences who would appreciate the latter might still go to see the film, while younger viewers are rather attracted by today's fast-paced cinema. This aspect is not to be disregarded, especially when looking at the visualization and style of direction of the remake.

Fig. 22. Above: the collapsed coach in the 2007 remake of *3:10 to Yuma*. Below: the same scene as it was to be seen in the original of 1956.

Since discussions of gender and ethnicity have caused due criticism of the genre's formula in general, and received greater attention especially in later Westerns (see above), these presently relevant aspects shall be focused on very briefly, before this analysis of *3:10 to Yuma* will be concluded. This recent Western does not employ any such tactics as *The Missing*, and does not consciously foreground issues of gender and race. Instead, *3:10 to Yuma* (2007) justifies its Euroamerican viewpoint behind the shield of faithfulness to the conventions of a classic genre, and historical accuracy in the depiction of a period, which was, apparently, racist and anti-feminist after all. What the audience is presented with is ultimately the perspective of characters that imagine the Apache as people that simply enjoy killing, whites who utter such statements as, "What we need is a negro to show these Chinese what real work is." The portrayal of Native Americans is obviously formulaic: a faceless, invisible threat, of which we literally do not get to see more than a few feathers and two barely perceivable faces (Fig. 23). Equally, the Chinese railroad builders are hardly more than mere props. Details like Wade's subliminal criticism of Byron's involvement in an Apache massacre, or the point-of-view shot of Will's encounter with a Chinese worker of his age (who is obviously in a worse situation than the rancher son, after all) show that the film is well aware of this stereotypical focus on Anglo characters, but it consciously avoids taking a more critical or revisionist stance. With regard to gender, it may only be pointed out that the director of the 1956 film has been called significantly "alien to the cult of machismo, to cynical manipulation," often making women characters his mouthpiece, challenging the film's heroes without hypocrisy or Puritanism (Tavernier 48). This contrasts with the suggestion that the original *3:10 to Yuma*, in which Dan takes initiative to regain his wife's respect, showed "how the Western had become a virility symbol for the female-dominated male in an urban society" (Skelsey). Skelsey conjectures that the remake of such a film, an indication that the Western is becoming popular again, might be a response to feminism.

Fig. 23. *3:10 to Yuma* (2007).

In conclusion, *3:10 to Yuma* (2007) takes a special position among the most recent Westerns, as it allows for the most direct comparison with a prominent film of the genre's heyday. The alteration of certain features from the original *3:10 to Yuma* might be relevant in the attempt to characterize the Western genre as it appears today. There is no doubt that this film was carefully chosen as the model for a large-scale Western remake, since it has been treated as one of the most remarkable and sophisticated of the classic Westerns. Hanisch claims that if one of the so-called psychological Westerns really deserves this label, it must be *3:10 to Yuma* (279), and Hembus argues that it degrades the celebrated *High Noon* to a matter of ridiculous and naive simplicity (*Lexikon* 750). Nevertheless, it has been shown that the remake deviates from the original in crucial points. Macnab argues that the alternated screenplay does "more to expand the scope of the story than to distort it," but this is disputable. So, Mangold's film not only makes Wade's character more ambiguous and Dan's more vulnerable, but exchanges the original theme of short-lived, selfless heroism for one of myth-creation, and adds an ideological emphasis on materialistic wealth as opposed to the pioneer ideology of the 1956 film. It is not entirely clear why these changes were made, and whether they have to be read as a revisionist approach to the formula Western. While the original itself does not exactly fit predefined formulaic patters (which might be an explanation why it was chosen for a remake), other striking deviations, like the elaborated action scenes and greater on-screen violence, might simply be explained by the efforts to adjust a classic film to modern standards and audiences. Beyond that, as Macnab notes, the remake does not foreground any contemporary references and is thus not to be seen as a mere allegory with topical resonance, but as a faithful representative of the Western genre. As such, it is a clear instance of Western nostalgia, trying to present the genre in a form which strongly associates it with the traditional Western, yet lives up to present-day standards (Macnab). Regardless of the innovations of the original *3:10 to Yuma*, Macnab is basically right when he calls the remake a "classical piece of storytelling with themes and characters that can be found in the very earliest Westerns," which incorporates all of the old archetypes and oppositions. This significant "return to old values" may be seen as the predominant motive of the makers of *3:10 to Yuma* (2007).

3.4. *The Assassination of Jesse James by the Coward Robert Ford*: A Myth Revisited

Andrew Dominik's *The Assassination of Jesse James by the Coward Robert Ford* is based on Ron Hansen's novel of the same name, and depicts the last years of famous real-life outlaw Jesse James' (Brad Pitt) life and his death in a documentary style, and with special emphasis on the role his assassin Bob Ford (Casey Affleck) played in the events. In Minnesota, in 1881, while Jesse James and his gang prepare for a train robbery, Bob Ford asks Jesse's brother Frank for a pivotal position in the gang, but is turned down. After the turbulent robbery, Bob approaches Jesse with similar intentions. Jesse derides the young man's idolatry for him, but eventually grants him the privilege to stay at his place for menial tasks; one more reason for the other gang members to make fun of Bob. Meanwhile, the outlaw develops an increasing, and not wholly unjustified paranoia about the disloyalty of his gang. He visits one of them, Ed Miller, and kills him. At the same time, two other gang members, ladykiller Dick Liddil and Jesse's cousin Wood Hite, get in conflict over Dick's sexual advances towards the young wife of Wood's father, while staying at the latter's house. It escalates in a chaotic gunfight in the house of Martha Bolton, in which Bob eventually kills Wood, who is buried sloppily in a nearby forest. When Jesse James comes by that house, Dick Liddil keeps himself hidden for fear of the outlaw, while Bob is humiliated both by his brother Charley and by Jesse for his obsessive worship of the latter during an uneasy dinner table conversation. Jesse then settles in St. Joseph with Charley, where he confesses to him how he killed Ed Miller, demanding a confession in return, but Charley keeps denying holding any secrets from him. The continuing degradation and humiliation of Bob Ford has taken its toll on him by now, and he decides to turn the James gang in to the authorities, starting with Dick Liddil. Charley then manages to convince Jesse to let Bob team up with them again for the next coup. They pick up Bob, and both Ford brothers move into Jesse's family's house, rather to the dislike of his suspicious wife Zee and their two children. Jesse's distrust of Bob surfaces in impulsive attacks on the young worshiper, but he finally seeks for conciliation in presenting Bob with a shiny revolver. Ultimately, seeing his task through with great concerted effort, Bob kills Jesse in his own house by shooting him through the head from the back with that same revolver, while the outlaw dusts a picture, with Charley standing by. After unconvincingly explaining to the distraught Zee that it was only an accident, they run off to the telegraph office to inform the authorities of the incident via wire. While the news of Jesse's death rapidly spread, while his body is photographed and his legendary status manifested, the Ford brothers put the assassination on stage, with Charley portraying Jesse and Bob himself. They become something of celebrities, but not enjoying the approval of the public, especially Bob. Guilt and superstition drive Charley into suicide. Isolated and anguished, Bob thrives on the hate of his contemporaries and is eventually assassinated himself in 1892 by a self-proclaimed avenger of Jesse James.

The plot and character patterns of *The Assassination* do obviously not match formulaic genre conventions. Weidinger notes that the film concentrates on the psychological drama of the characters, but does not foreground a traditional Western story and thus lacks a real narrative focus ("Re: Nationale Mythen"). Considering the attempts, or at least claims of former Jesse James films to reproduce actual events in the life of a historical figure, one may conclude that none of these is a formulaic Western in the narrow sense, since historical facts are unlikely to overlap with genre conventions. Nevertheless, films like Henry King's classic *Jesse James* (1939) are considered epitomes of the Western genre, and Jesse James himself is seen as one of the most vibrant figures that shaped the myth of the Wild West. Why Jesse's personality lends itself to a paradigmatic

Western protagonist becomes obvious when considering a number of aspects. The extreme instance of individualism that such idealized outlaws represent is central to the myth of the West, and as they are positioned between self-interest and social responsibility, corresponding to wilderness and civilization, they are similarly defined as the traditional Western hero (Saunders 64). A "social bandit" like Jesse James corresponds to the Western hero in the way that both ultimately fail or only partially succeed in a world where their culturally defined masculine virtues are no longer effective (White 235) (The label "social bandit," widely used to describe sympathetic Robin Hood-like outlaw figures (see above), was coined by Hobsbawm to define bandits whom circumstances have forced to become such, who are protected by the community, who supposedly serve a higher justice although they violate a law, and who can only die or be captured when betrayed (qtd. in White 222)). White points out correctly that the Western genre in itself is not a "simple-minded celebration of the triumph of American virtue over evil," but a play on unresolved oppositions and contradictions of American culture (235), and one such contradiction is the parallel despair and optimism of the frontier which the Jesse James myth personifies (Bell). That Western heroes and social bandits--ultimately social failures--enjoy such great appeal among audiences, gives insight into the paradoxes of American culture (White 222, 236). Finally, it shall be implied that the actual events in Jesse James' life have generally been distorted for the sake of myth-creating accounts, occasionally to such a degree that the formulaic character complex "savages-hero-townspeople," as suggested by Cawelti (see above), is well represented by a "railroaders/Pinkerton detectives-James gang-agricultural south" relation in many Jesse James films. In sum, we might consider films around the famous outlaw almost exclusively as Westerns, even if some are on the verge of history films, or deviate from the formula for the sake of historicity. So, in order to shed light on the characteristics of the recent Western as such, *The Assassination*, as the most up-to-date Jesse James film, needs to be considered from the background of older films centering on this mythical figure.

Not surprisingly, cinema has found many ways to canonize Jesse, either by rectifying his crimes in their relation to the "crimes" of authorities, by depicting him as wholly innocent, or by idolizing him as a rebel in the mid-fifties trend set by Marlon Brando and James Dean (Hembus, *Geschichte* 545-6). Henry King's *Jesse James*, mentioned above, focuses on the attempted bank raid by Frank and Jesse James and their gang at Northfield Minnesota as the turning point of their fortunes, and consolidated the fame of the brothers as screen heroes (Saunders 63). Apologetic of character ("I don't think America is ashamed of Jesse James," his funeral address will finally say), it twists actualities to morally justify Jesse's crimes. Elements like the raid on the James farm which leaves their mother dead and introduces the James brothers into crime, have some historical foundation, but are obviously distorted (Saunders 66). The film presents itself as historically authentic, and claims that the scriptwriter worked of the basis of research which involved collaboration with Jesse James' actual granddaughter, who, however, denied herself that her grandfather had much in common with the Jesse in the film (Hembus, *Lexikon* 343). Tuska puts it bluntly when he says the film is "totally misrepresenting all major issues and personalities" (141). But while the largest part of the film has supporting characters repeatedly assuring Jesse of the righteousness of his act, claiming he not only has the right, but the duty of revenge, or praising him for his braveness to defend himself, the latter part of the film is not entirely uncritical. Jesse loses control and gets involved in more raids than the film's moral structure allows, and eventually he loses the support and affirmation of his contemporaries: "He ain't a knight anymore, fighting the bad railroad. He's a wild animal." As King's film is often seen as the epitome of Jesse James films, and *The Assassination* focuses so much on the character of Bob Ford, it shall be added here that in this classic film Jesse's assassin still fits all the negative stereotypes the myth demands. Jesse's epitaph, calling Bob a "traitor and coward whose name is not worth mentioning here," is uninhibitedly stressed, and suggests that the film's ideology supports that opinion. At the first opportunity to kill Jesse that offers itself to Bob, he lacks the courage to see the job through, and an extreme close-up frames what Saunders calls a "pop-eyed mixture of greed and fear" (68). This flat depiction is obviously a long way from Casey Affleck's intricate portrayal of Bob in *The Assassination*. According to Leonardy, interpretations that break with the tradition of such euphemistic social bandit images make Jesse a sly, unscrupulous, mentally and morally defective man, who deserves no sympathy (138). Among the works Leonardy discusses, such a harsh description probably fits best the novel by Ron Hansen, on which *The Assassination* is based. But the latter film is certainly not the first to take a deconstructive approach towards the popular myth. *The Great Northfield Minnesota Raid* (1971) is often quoted as a significant revisionist take on the events around the bank robbery which was also central to the 1939 film. "Addressed to a more knowing and cynical age," it relegates Jesse to a supporting role, gives Cole Younger the top billing instead, and, when the voice-over promises the "true story" of the fateful event, it signals its own rhetoric rather than a serious claim to belief (Saunders 69-70). A combination of imaginative freedom and practical realism determines this film's subversive and satirical relationship to earlier films; it is deliberately not closer to the recoverable historical truth than Henry King's film (Saunders 71, 75). Walter Hill's *The Long Riders* (1980) then meant a step back from the early seventies' disillusionment to an again more positive image of the bandit (see above). Leonardy criticizes the film as idealizing a clichéd Jesse, not questioning his role and motives, and lacking new approaches (125). It revives the simplified patterns of King's film, and although the postwar Missouri is finely visualized as the historical background, the film's excessive violence is an unsuccessful attempt to create realism (Leonardy 125). Released in 1980, the proverbial year of the Western's death, it fared badly at the box office (Hembus, *Lexikon* 398; see above). The list of Jesse James films released to this day could go on for much longer, and make wonder which perspective on the myth and treatment of the matter on has not yet been employed. Almost 60 years before *The Assassination*, *I Shot Jesse James* (1948) was a film that already focused on the Bob Ford character, and was shot by Samuel Fuller, a director who apparently neither liked Westerns, nor the character of Jesse James (Hembus, *Lexikon* 321). Even more recently than Walter Hill's film, the elegiac and contemplative *The Last Days of Frank and Jesse James* (1986) tried to present a new view by concentrating on a period in the life of the outlaws which is generally disregarded in most Jesse James films, as it lacks the foundation for fast-paced action scenes.

Fig. 24. Left: Casey Affleck as Robert Ford in *The Assassination*. Right: the real Robert Ford, posing with the gun with which he shot Jesse James. Photograph (from Leonardy 233).

So, what innovations, if any, set *The Assassination* off against former films to justify its release? As viewers' demands for authenticity increase, and since most former Jesse James films seemingly fail to live up to their claims for historical accuracy, one might expect new approaches in this direction here. Indeed, Kitses notes the wealth of information and period detail the film offers ("Twilight" 19), and Buscombe praises its good feel for the Victorian milieu in decor, fashions, and speech patterns (*Assassination*). So it seems that *The Assassination* makes noteworthy attempts at authenticity where possible--which basically means in its outer appearance. Casey Affleck's resemblance to the actual Bob Ford is remarkable (Fig. 24), and although co-producer Brad Pitt was arguably cast for promotional reasons rather than for his resemblance to the real Jesse, some scenes manage to frame him in a way evocative of historical photographs (Fig. 25)--most impressively, of course, when the picture of Jesse's dead body is being taken. On the other hand, in the depiction of most events, reliable historical accounts are not as easily accessible. Since the earliest hour, and while Jesse was still alive, reality and fantasy strongly overlapped in the documentation of the outlaw's turbulent life (Leonardy 106). In *Major Problem in the History of the American West*, Milner, Butler, and Lewis present a popular document by a contemporary, who recounts the events around Jesse's death in great detail, and, not surprisingly, with the claim for absolute accuracy (197-8). As can be imagined, the omniscient style of narration renders it duly unreliable; the author even seems to be able to know what is going on in the minds of the involved, and describes details nobody else but they could know of (Milner, Butler, and Lewis 197-8). Nevertheless, such "dramatic accounts akin to pulp fiction," as Milner, Butler, and Lewis aptly describe them (196), are the required means to reproduce events as close to actual fact as possible, and their inspiration can be sensed in the depiction of Jesse's death, the crowding around his house, and the taking of the photograph of his body in *The Assassination*. Ultimately, though, the makers may be given credit for having come to a similar conclusion as Robert Benton, who denounces the attempts of later Western filmmakers to proclaim "this is how it really was," as nonsense (qtd. in Hembus, *Lexikon* 343). Benton says it is irrelevant how it really was, and nobody seems to know exactly anyhow (qtd. in Hembus, *Lexikon* 343). In this spirit, Ron Hansen and the makers of *The Assassination* have based the narration on what historical detail could be found, and, as will be seen, used it as a frame for an innovative character study plastered with creative imagination, but without the euphemistic or idealizing motives of earlier films.

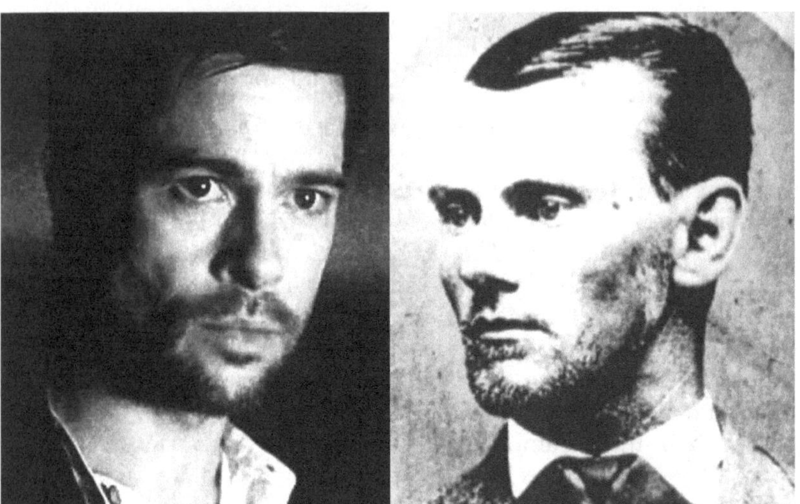

Fig. 25. Left: Brad Pitt as Jesse James in *The Assassination*. Right: portrait of the actual Jesse James (1847-1882). Photograph (from Leonardy 226).

But with the obvious lack of accurate documentation, it has never been a mystery that a portrayal of Jesse James in film or fiction always leaves room for interpretation. Any such depiction of the legendary outlaw is then defined by its relative closeness or distance to the mythical social bandit figure of Jesse, which has been manifested in popular culture early on, especially by the sympathizing newspaper editor John Newman Edwards, who transfigured Jesse already during his lifetime by such eulogies as the following:

> "He never boasts [...]. He speaks low, is polite, deferential and accommodating. He does not kill save in stubborn self-defense. He has nothing in common with a murderer. He hates the highwaymen and the coward. He is an outlaw, but he is not a criminal, no matter what prejudiced public opinion may declare or malignant partisans [sic] dislike make noisy with reiteration." (qtd. in Leonardy 108)

While Henry King's *Jesse James* would be an instance of a portrayal of Jesse relatively faithful to these idealized attributes, *The Great Northfield Minnesota Raid*, for example, clearly deconstructs the myth, and so does *The Assassination*. Since Kitses underlines the film's faithfulness to its literary model ("Twilight" 20), most of Leonardy's comments on Hansen's book hereafter will also apply to the film; as, for example, when he notes that the narration reproduces Jesse's crimes without taking sides, and describes the depiction of the outlaw as that of an infantile, emotionally disturbed psychopath, with a behavioral disorder and atavistic features (125, 127). Brad Pitt's Jesse James is just that, and his unstable and contradictory behavior patterns, his impulsiveness, irresponsibility, craving for recognition, vanity, insecurity, fearsomeness, hypersensitivity, cunning, irrationality, prudery, sanctimoniousness, and sadism make him arguably the darkest and most uncanny Jesse James in film history, matching none of Hobsbawm's criteria of the knightly social bandit (Leonardy 125-6). But instead of making him a faceted, complex round character, this overflow of contradictory attributes really leaves him short of any identity. An extended dissolve of the approaching Jesse on horseback from Ed Miller's point of view lets him appear like a translucent ghost rider; he is merely a projection by the *potpourri* of discrepant bandits and crooks surrounding him, first and foremost Bob Ford (Fig. 26). Buscombe brings it to the point when he describes him as a "hollow man, [...] a character of tics and mannerisms, but no inner life. No one really knows Jesse--which enables those around him to project onto him whatever they seek" (*Assassination*). This can be read as the film's essential revisionist comment on the Jesse James myth: in whatever way the countless accounts of Jesse James' life have portrayed and characterized him, all of them are merely imaginary projections onto a historical figure, whose true personality and identity must remain a mystery and unknown. The solution to the problem, and the answer to the quest for the identity of the man behind the myth, is probably given by Bob, when he reminds his brother Charley: "he's just a human being." The final revisionism of the Jesse James saga is then seen by Kitses in the scene of the actual assassination ("Twilight" 20). The demonstrativeness with which Jesse lays down his guns, and his idleness when he sees Bob's reflection in the picture, propose a significant break with the regular conception of Jesse's death: here, it is a kind of suicide (Kitses, "Twilight" 20).

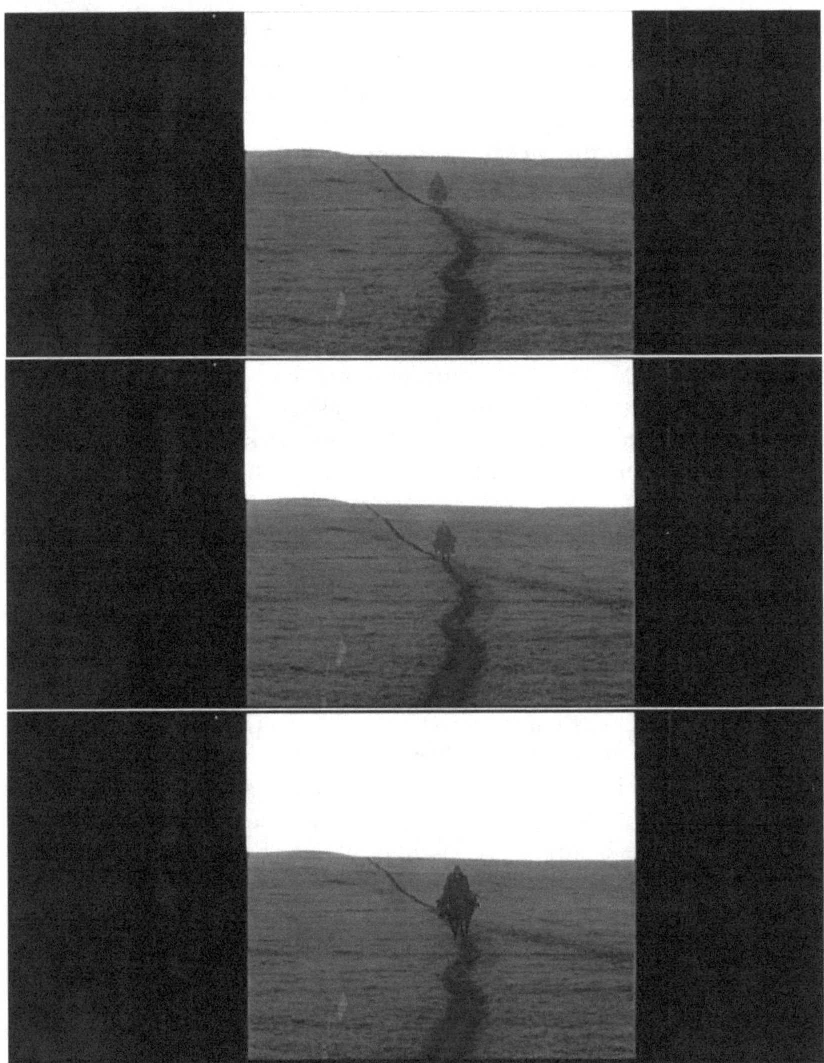

Fig. 26. *The Assassination of Jesse James by the Coward Robert Ford.*

The other more striking aspect of *The Assassination* in comparison to manifold previous film adaptations is the shift of focus to the Bob Ford character, respectively the relationship Ford-James, that of a teenage admirer to his grown-up idol (Weidinger, "Re: Nationale Mythen"). When Jesse is framed motionless in a rocking chair, with the expression and posture that give him the "aloof and commanding air of royalty," the viewer may sense why the callow Bob strives for a "sidekick" status (Kitses, "Twilight" 16) (Fig. 27). He admires the man he knows from the already existing legend of the social bandit obsessively, and the stubbornness with which he adheres to an ideal of which both he and Jesse know that it is fantasy ("They're all lies, you know," Jesse tell Bob about the stories surrounding him: the young man nods in approval), make him a deformed character as well (Leonardy 126). Bob later expresses his feeling of inferiority and craving for recognition clearly when he explains: "I've been a nobody all my life. I was the baby [...], the one people picked on" (Leonardy 126), but the viewer notices his dilemma from the first time on he opens his mouth to introduce himself to Frank James, which is instantly greeted by muffled, distant laughter. But, having hero-worshipped the outlaw from an early age, he is ready to suffer derision and contempt as long as it gets him closer to Jesse and enables him to absorb some of his fame (Buscombe, *Assassination*). However, realizing the incompatibility of the increasingly paranoid real Jesse with his idealized projection, and having repeatedly experienced humiliation and disregard by his idol (Jesse repeatedly expresses his disinterest in the young man's affairs by suddenly changing the subject in conversations, or simply ignoring him), his disposition changes. The viewer witnesses Bob's "hopes for glory with Jesse changing focus [...], his sycophancy and hero-worship metamorphosing into hatred" (Kitses, "Twilight" 18). In the end, an isolated, retrospective Bob tells his only female companion, a dance-hall singer, that it was fear of being killed himself and the reward money that drove him to assassinate Jesse--but the audience knows better by then that these were exactly not his reasons. His plan of assassination was carried out for the moment of notoriety it would bring, and not surprisingly, he becomes an object of contempt as the celebrity palls (Buscombe, *Assassination*). Hence, while former film adaptations of the Jesse James myth focus either on the outlaw's famed exploits, or, at best, interrogate the social significance of his criminal career, Andrew Dominik's film poses a novelty in concentrating on the "motivations of those who brought about his downfall" (Buscombe, *Assassination*).

Fig. 27. *The Assassination of Jesse James by the Coward Robert Ford.*

The Jesse James myth seems so deeply rooted in the American mind that it is unlikely to ever see a "final" Jesse James film, just as there will never be a "final" Hamlet adaptation, for example. As Buscombe points out correctly, each generation chooses its own interpretation of a Jesse James to suit its time, as has been shown in the brief listing of various adaptations above (*Assassination*). Changes in cinema audiences and society can be a determining factor for the film industry's output, and the modification of a popular outlaw figure which has been part of the Western genre since its earliest days may illustrate these changes vividly (Saunders 63). *The Assassination* might prove especially significant with regard to the present time as a "study of celebrity culture," as Buscombe calls it (*Assassination*). The themes of hero-worship and paranoia that run through Dominik's film seem appropriate to our present time, which Kitses somewhat bitterly describes as follows:

> "[D]ominated [...] by the media's ugly assassination of celebrities, the deranged behaviour of damaged souls who hunger for recognition, and pundits who encourage our worst instincts--envy, greed, morbid curiosity and malicious pleasure in the downfall of the mighty." ("Twilight" 16)

Bob Ford's character, described by Kitses as a groupie and stalker "ahead of his time" ("Twilight" 18), is marked by a pathological lust for fame and an unshakable and insolent faith in his exceptional abilities and in "being chosen" for greatness: "I honestly believe I'm destined for great things," he tells Frank James blatantly. When Jesse asks the 19-year-old about his age, he senses his naive overestimation of his own capabilities peculiar to teenagers, and is promptly confirmed in it when he inquires further, "You feel older than that, though, don't you?"--Bob answers with a smile of false embarrassment: "Yes, I do." He has a similar facial expression when Charley calls on him to tell Jesse of the many things they have in common, one of Bob's childhood fantasies that resulted from his exaggerated identification with the outlaw (Fig. 28). He knows it is presumptuous and embarrassing, but he still believes in the meaningfulness of these facts, and is tempted to let Jesse know.[16] Of course, Jesse is hardly impressed, and instead mocks his dreamy admirer. But such setbacks are hard to take for Bob, and when his supposed calling for fame and greatness are put in question or not acknowledged, he gets cross, such as here, or when he is told to leave a ball he is trying to attend, go upstairs, and hide his identity--being told he is not "the goddamn belle of the ball." But his faith in himself remains steadfast for the longest time, as he regularly finds confirmation for his alleged skills, filling him with pride that borders on arrogance, and a demand for recognition. Eager for applause, his proud smile when he manages to catch Jesse off guard early in the film is the same as when he hands the note to the telegrapher saying he just killed Jesse James. Shortly after he has shot Wood through the back of the head much like he will do with Jesse later, there is no sign of remorse of his face; instead he smiles patronizingly, twirling his Colt somewhat clumsily (he will manage to do this better when he declares after each staging of Jesse's assassination, "And this is how I killed Jesse James"). The lesson that Bob should have learned is simple: Jesse brings it to the point when Charley Ford assures him that his younger brother thinks highly of him, replying: "All of America does." When Bob finally learns this lesson that he is only one among many who think themselves special, and that not every measure to acquire fame is worth to be taken, it is too late. Ten years after the assassination he confesses how much he regrets having killed Jesse, sitting in his apartment lonely all day, "flipping over playing cards, looking at his destiny in every king and jack." Even after his death, the film's narrator tells us, Bob will not experience the fame, notoriety, and appraisal of the social bandit Jesse James. Kitses says: "Such plays on the theme of the struggle of common men to be heard may resonate with audiences of today, when many in the US feel they live in dark times ruled over by small minds" ("Twilight" 20). While the message of *The Assassination* in this regard seems to be a pessimistic one to all appearances, it remains two-fold: after all, Bob Ford has acquired some posthumous fame with this film.

Fig. 28. *The Assassination of Jesse James by the Coward Robert Ford.*

In sum, *The Assassination* stands out among other Jesse James films in that it does not euphemistically transfigure the myth, but, like Ron Hansen's novel on which the script is based, interrogate it (Leonardy 138). In contrast to the stable and pastoral America of Henry King's *Jesse James*, for example, the world of Dominik's film is a more mysterious one of more substantial forces, fates, and destinies; and the baldness of the title obviously belies the complex tragic action (Kitses, "Twilight" 18). To the revisionist ambitions in recent Westerns we have seen so far, like women, Native Americans, or heroism, *The Assassination* adds the deconstruction of a central Western myth, that of the social bandit Jesse James. As such, the genre's traditional action conventions are sacrificed to an interior drama, often conveyed beneath the surface (Kitses, "Twilight" 16). Based on historical facts, but completed by creative fiction, it recounts the plunge of Jesse's last gang into distrust and destruction, eventually becoming an unsparing study of the psyches and characters of the outlaws and the prevailing circumstances of the time (Kitses, "Twilight" 16; Leonardy 138). The film's careful and detailed visualization, aimed at historical accuracy, and the yearning sadness and reflectiveness that surround the American icon Jesse James at times in this film, suggest some sense of Western nostalgia. However, we have to concede that Kitses is right when he compares *The Assassination* to the works of the American director of revisionist Westerns *per se*, Sam Peckinpah, observing that Dominik's film is nowhere "guilty of that director's [Peckinpah] elegiac yearning for the romance of the West" ("Twilight" 19). Here, there are no heroes (Kitses, "Twilight" 19), not even tragic anti-heroes, so this makes *The Assassination* a deconstructionist Western for the largest part.

4. The Western of our Time: Conclusion and Outlook

This paper has analyzed the most recent representatives of a film genre which has reflected and shaped American culture for more than hundred years. It has aimed to illuminate what ideological biases, narrative structures, treatments of established Western myths, and commentary on gender, ethnicity, morality, and the present sociocultural context characterize the most significant Westerns of late. The year 2000 has been laid down as an arbitrary lower boundary, and the films released between this year and the moment of writing, were considered as "recent" Westerns. A preliminary chapter has provided essential background information on historicity in the Western genre, on the history of the genre itself, and on the major films of late which may be counted as Westerns. The first paragraph of that chapter has indicated that the relation between the portrayal of historical events, figures, and settings and actual facts is highly problematic. In spite of often made claims for accuracy and generally welcomed ambitions of filmmakers in that direction, especially in the later decades of the twentieth century, it is advisable to maintain a critical stance towards supposedly historically authentic Westerns. In the second paragraph it has been shown that the history of the American Western may be divided into epochs, which are characterized by common ideological, traditionalist, or revisionist features in the films of these times. It has also been seen that the development of the Western over a hundred years has been marked by great fluctuation in annual output, popularity, sophistication and relevance. The most recent Westerns, which have been introduced in the third paragraph, point to a relative unpopularity of the genre at the present day, concluding from the total number of films. Subtracting Civil War films and several notable pro-, neo-, or post-Westerns, the remaining instances set in the narrower historical context of the classic Western are even fewer. Nevertheless, most are distinguished by thematic innovation, high production value, and individualistic design.

Chapter three has then investigated four example films, which have been chosen for their outstanding critical renown, commercial success, and their deliberately creative dissection of the genre, in close analysis. They were examined for formulaic settings, character alignments and action patterns, as well as for their basic ideological attitude, unconventional narrative devices and structures, and innovative filming techniques. Aspects like costume, set design, choice of cast, photography, etc. were neither disregarded. The analysis has shown that the genre still has potential to generate artistically significant films, oriented to classic Western themes, but nevertheless showing great variety and individualism. It is exactly in this sense, that one crucial question still needs to be answered, though. In chapter two, the history of the genre has been chronologically divided into certain eras whose films share common features and themes. So, do the major Westerns released since the year 2000 also all go in similar directions, or are they marked by strong contrasts? Can universal motifs and ideologies be traced, or rather a basic individualism and variety? Throughout this paper it has been assumed that there are two fundamental, opposing aspects that might characterize a Western today: deconstruction and nostalgia. The term deconstruction here refers to deliberate breaks with traditional genre conventions, to revisionism and innovative novelties. In opposition to that, traditionalism, the adherence to formulaic conventions, an elegiac sense for obsolete frontier values, and obvious references to Western classics have been united under the heading nostalgia. Paying special attention to this, this concluding chapter will recapitulate the findings of the investigations of the four example films, in order to make a comparison between the films which might shed light on whether there is such a thing as the "Western of our time," or whether these works have to be seen as isolated cases. Following that, the common opinion that the Western genre is basically "dead" and would therefore not be able to lay claims on a continuing existence in whatever form, will briefly be considered.

The first of the four example films, *Open Range* (2003), is clearly on the traditionalist, nostalgic side. It presents an original Western plot which adheres to the Western formula in both character alignment and narrative action. The few novel elements are subtle, and can hardly be called revisionist, like the attempts to depict violence more realistically, or the female lead above the age of the average Western heroine. This, however, is one of the aspects where *The Missing* (2003) takes a crucially different stance. In its female main character, this film tries to portray an emancipated frontier woman, yet within the boundaries of realism and authenticity. Its objective is to deconstruct the traditional role of women in the Western, and it is, to the greatest part, successful in this respect. In addition to that, it aims to continue a line of revisionist Westerns which had its first climax in the early seventies: "Indian sympathy" films. Next to the Western's traditional anti-feminism, its racist tendencies have been a major point of criticism, and a reason for the genre's decline. Attempts at an accurate depiction of nineteenth century Apache culture, and the avoidance of a black-and-white moral division in any direction between

Euroamericans and Native Americans are the main tactics *The Missing* employs to deconstruct the negative image of Indians, which is undeniably inherent in the classic Western. Even though an Anglocentric bias is still discernible, *The Missing* has to be noted for these revisionist motives, which are almost completely absent in *Open Range*, where the female protagonist is only defined through her interaction with men, and where Native American characters are not involved at all. What the two films nevertheless share is a formulaic basic substance; not only *Open Range*, but also *The Missing* has a classic tripartite character division, and a paradigmatic Western plot structure of chase and pursuit. However, the round Native American and women characters are still the most remarkable elements of the latter film, and director Ron Howard clearly has a point when he expresses his hope that these aspects offer a "way to take a fresh perspective on that [the frontier] period." With this in mind, and following a nineties wave of "Indian sympathy" Western and some "women Westerns,"[17] one would probably have expected more Westerns along the lines of *The Missing* in recent years. However, they are rare, and Howard's film stands alone among relevant newer Western productions as a film that makes Native Americans and feminist issues a central topic. Like in *Open Range*, such themes are dismissed in another major Western of late, in *3:10 to Yuma* (2007), where Native Americans have only an infinitesimal relevance to the plot, and a male universe is the action's framework. The release of this film may be read as an indication that a traditionalist approach as Kevin Costner employed has ultimately more appeal to filmmakers than Ron Howard's deconstructive one. First and foremost, *3:10 to Yuma* (2007) is notable as the remake of one outstanding Western classic. Admittedly, it has some revisionist character as such; on the one hand the original itself was unconventional (among other aspects in the characterization of its protagonist), and on the other hand the remake is not wholly faithful to the model in essential ways. But as it deliberately evokes the traditional Western not only in reprising a definite classic, but also in its visualization and incorporation of archetypal elements of the genre, it clearly positions itself on the nostalgic end. This can not as easily be said about the fourth Western in consideration, *The Assassination of Jesse James by the Coward Robert Ford* (2007). Unlike *The Missing*, it is neither concerned with the role of women, nor that of Native Americans in the Western film. But what unites the two films is their deconstruction of traditional Western elements: in *The Assassination* it is obviously that of a mythical figure of the West, Jesse James. While essentially a violent film, it neither shares *3:10 to Yuma*'s Western typical emphasis on spectacular action scenes, nor *Open Range*'s naivety and simplicity, and eventually it sets itself off against *The Missing* by a completely non-formulaic plot pattern. However, this most "intellectual" Western of the foursome must not be disregarded, and not at last its critical success makes it one of the most remarkable recent Westerns.

While these four films are probably the most significant Westerns among later years, they are obviously not the only ones. In chapter two a number of films have been introduced, which must not be ignored when trying to characterize the genre at the present day, because, after all, these comprise the "Western of our time," together with the films above. For the lack of room, though, only those three of them which are Westerns in the closest sense shall briefly be reconsidered here. *Seraphim Falls* (2006) is noteworthy for its simplistic, yet appealing form and realization. Notably, it seems to go hand in hand with the nostalgia of *Open Range* and *3:10 to Yuma*, for its inclusion of many traditional Western features. On the other side, and not unlike *3:10 to Yuma* as well, it interrogates the conventional good-bad division, and some innovative, though not revolutionary elements prevent it from becoming a naive matter. *The Proposition* (2004) is certainly a revisionist Western, being not even set in America, but Australia, and presenting a mixture of poetic elegy and an Australian frontier of violence, oppression, and hostility, brazenly exposed. Still, its visualization, character alignment and major narrative patterns are made up of Western archetypes and topoi, and the Australian frontier shows elementary parallels to the American West that make is basically the same setting differently furnished. The television series *Deadwood* (2004-6) unites nostalgic and deconstructive elements, in that it claims to accurately represent historical figures, events and settings, but renders the West as a depraved and grimy den of iniquity, nearly devoid of such traditionally highly estimated values as morality and righteousness.

Inferring from these facts, it would seem rash to try to formulate a framework of dominant themes, characteristics and ideologies, universally applicable to all significant Westerns of recent years. Obviously the relatively small number of Western productions consists of highly individualist works, and common influences and motivations can only be speculated about. Perhaps this much sought-after grail, the main characteristic of the recent Western, has already been found in the peculiar diversity and individualism. Not at last, many of the late Western and pro-Westerns owe their existence to independent production companies, or the very personal involvement and ambition of individuals with an apparent soft spot for the Western, such as Billy Bob Thornton, Nick Cave (who also made the music for *The Assassination*, besides that for *The Proposition*, of which he also wrote the script), Tommy Lee Jones, Kevin Costner, or Ronald F. Maxwell (whose "Civil War trilogy," including the recent *Gods and Generals* (2002) appears to be a very personal project), which already says something about Western nostalgia in itself. But it would also be wrong to proclaim that the Westerns of recent years have nothing in common at all. The two poles of "deconstruction" and "nostalgia" might be misleading here, as most films turn out to be located somewhere in the middle between them. So maybe it is this unification of revisionist and traditionalist elements which marks the present-day Western. And while revisionism and deconstruction are certainly prominent features in a great part of these Western, especially in *The Missing* or *The Assassination*, it seems to be the nostalgic element (most vividly in *Open Range* and *3:10 to Yuma*) which has the potential to set the recent Western apart from, for example, that of the nineties: revisionism and deconstruction were already a predominant feature then. Especially the reexamination of ethnicity and gender in the Western of the foregoing decade has tapered off, with *The Missing* being the only noteworthy exception of recent years--whether for the better or the worse so, remains to be seen.[18] In addition to that, the many references to established Western classics observable in most of the films point to a nostalgic attitude towards more traditional Western values.

In any case, the later years may not have generated an overly number of Western releases, but the lack in quantity is made up for with quality and innovation. Hence, such recurring predictions of the death of the Western as Macnab mentions are thwarted, and Kitses adds that complaints that the Western has been killed off ignore such works as *The Three Burials of Melquiades Estrada* (2005), *Deadwood*, and *Brokeback Mountain* (2005) ("Days of the Dead" 18). The Western seems to have as firm a position in American culture as the social bandit Jesse James has in frontier mythology, and this is confirmed by the fact that Westerns centering on this outlaw present novel views and interpretations of the legend at least every decade, with *The Assassination* being only the most recent instant. But to express some optimism about the special significance of the present-day Western, it may be suspected that it will take some time until a Jesse James film can top this one in innovative complexity and artistic relevance. Kitses, who says that the Western "never goes away," argues that "few have cause as much anticipation" as *The Assassination* ("Twilight" 16).

So, if the Western is still alive and kicking, how can this stubborn perseverance of a basically backwards oriented genre, constructed around a conservative value system, be explained and justified from a sociocultural perspective? The release of *Open Range*, closely following September Eleventh, lets Last conjecture that "the Western, with its traditional values and homespun heroics, can offer a way forward after the recent traumas--characterised by Charley's past--of a tarnished American dream" ("Western Values"). In the same film, the suppression of violence forced on the headlong protagonist may be a commentary on "America's incumbent cowboy leader and his aggressive and vengeful policies" (Kitses, "Forgiven" 24). To Kitses, the clustered release of the Westerns *3:10 to Yuma* and *The Assassination*, and the pro-Western *No Country for Old Men* (2007) is both significant and welcome; he notes that the myths and rituals of the Western have served the American public well in earlier troubled times: "if film-makers and audiences continue to be drawn to them, perhaps it's because the genre still has something to say about the nation's past that we need to hear" ("Twilight" 20). In that sense, the Western genre apparently continues to function as a crucial allegory to contemporary happenings in American society and culture by relating them to events in the nation's turbulent history.

Notes

[1] See, for example, the divisions in Fenin and Everson, or Seeßlen and Weil.

[2] The film *Smoke Signals* (1998), written, directed, and produced by Native Americans, and based on an episode from the book *The Lone Ranger and Tonto Fistfight in Heaven* (1994) by Native American author Sherman Alexie, picks up this issue in a humorous scene. One of the main characters, a proud and angry young man instructs another one, nerdy and talkative, on how to behave and act like an Indian: he is supposed to get stoic and look proud, as if he was to go hunting buffalo. Upon this, the other points out that their tribe never used to hunt buffalo, but were fishermen.

[3] The notorious outlaw-duo Butch Cassidy and Sundance Kid were still at large and wanted when the film came out, and in 1901, for example, the Dalton brothers had seized 33.000 dollars in two train robberies (Hanisch 20).

[4] A similar development can be observed in Eastwood's earlier film, *High Plains Drifter* (Smith, Paul 50).

[5] See, for example, Sandra Uebbing's *Amerika (er-)finden*, or Ulrich Bruckner's *Für ein paar Leichen mehr*. The pioneer in the study of the Italian Western was Christopher Frayling with his standard work *Spaghetti Westerns*, and his much acknowledged biography of Sergio Leone, *Something to Do with Death*.

[6] Hembus ascribes such a great significance to *The Searchers* that it is the one single film in his *Western-Lexikon* which is marked by four "stars" in the system of assessment he uses to evaluate the film-historical relevance of each entry (563). As initially defined in the book, the system should only distinguish between none, one, two, or three stars.

[7] Kilpatrick calls *Dead Man* the only Western at the time of her writing which manages to avoid the major Native American stereotypes (246). For more on the significance of *Dead Man*, see Szalosky.

[8] On the other hand, films like the most famous Civil War account *Gone With the Wind* (1939), are not.

[9] For Australian frontier violence, see, for example, Raymond Evans article "'Plenty Shoot 'Em': The Destruction of Aboriginal Societies along the Queensland Frontier" and others in Moses.

[10] For more on the role and function of landscape in the Western, see, for example, chapter three in Tompkins.

[11] For the relationship between television and feature film Westerns, see Boddy.

[12] Compare *Open Range*'s Sue here, who fits the attributes of a typical "blond."

[13] On the other hand, Evans suggests that the late thirties were already ahead of the forties and fifties in terms of female emancipation (211).

[14] While it would certainly be revealing to conduct a similar research project with a showing of *The Missing* instead of a considerably old film like *The Searchers*, it shall be pointed out that after all, Thomson accuses the former film of not having got sufficiently ahead of models like the latter in many relevant aspects.

[15] For more on the explicitness of the Italian Western's violence in contrast to the earlier American Western, see *Denn sie kannten kein Erbarmen*.

[16] Affleck's masterly performance as Bob has been justly praised by Buscombe here, as his face "expresses both the humiliations heaped upon him and the hunger for fame that drives him on" (*Assassination*). Eventually, Affleck won an Academy Award for the role.

[17] Among these, the most widely recognized films are *Ballad of Little Jo* (1993), *The Quick and the Dead* (1995), and also the television Western series *Dr. Quinn* (1993-8). It needs to be stressed, though, that *The Missing* is not to be pigeonholed as one of these; Weidinger notes that it does not present itself as a stereotyped "women Western" (*Nationale Mythen* 154; see above).

[18] One may only hope that filmmakers have not recently acquired a similar attitude as Paul Schrader attributes to Sam Peckinpah when he made *The Wild Bunch* (1969), supposedly saying, "Look, I know this is anachronism, I know this is fascist, I know this is sexist. I know this is evil and out-of-date. But God help me, I love it so" (qtd. in "Sam Peckinpah's West").

Works Cited

Films

The Alamo. Dir. John Wayne. Wayne/Batjac, 1960.

The Alamo. Dir. John Lee Hancock. 2004.

All the Pretty Horses. Dir. Billy Thornton. Columbia, 2000.

The Assassination of Jesse James by the Coward Robert Ford. Dir. Andrew Dominik. Perf. Brad Pitt and Casey Affleck. Warner, 2007.

Back to the Future Part III. Dir. Robert Zemeckis. Amblin, 1990.

The Ballad of Little Jo. Dir. Maggie Greenwald. Joco, 1993.

Batman Begins. Dir. Christopher Nolan. Warner, 2005.

Black Robe. Dir. Bruce Beresford. 1991.

Blueberry. Dir. Jan Kounen. Ajoz, 2004.

Brokeback Mountain. Dir. Ang Lee. Focus, 2005.

Broken Arrow. Dir. Delmer Daves. 20th Century Fox, 1950.

Broken Trail. Dir. Walter Hill. Butcher's Run, 2006.

Bronco Billy. Dir. Clint Eastwood. Warner, 1980.

Buffalo Bill and the Indians. Dir. Robert Altman. Laurentiis, 1976.

Butch Cassidy and the Sundance Kid. Dir. George Roy Hill. 1969.

Cold Mountain. Dir. Anthony Minghella. Miramax, 2003.

Dances With Wolves. Dir. Kevin Costner. Majestic, 1990.

Dead Man. Dir. Jim Jarmusch. 1995.

Deadwood. Dir. Edward Bianchi et al. HBO, 2004-6.

Deadwood: The Complete Second Season. Dir. Edward Bianchi et al. DVD. HBO, 2006.

Devil's Doorway. Anthony Mann. MGM, 1950.

Dr. Quinn. Dir. Alan J. Levi et al. CBS Television, 1993-8.

First Blood. Dir. Ted Kotcheff. Kassar/Vajna, 1981.

A Fistful of Dollars. Dir. Sergio Leone. 1964.

For a Few Dollars More. Dir. Sergio Leone. P.E.A., 1965.

Gods and Generals. Dir. Ronald F. Maxwell. Turner, 2002.

Gone With the Wind. Dir. Victor Fleming. Selznick International, 1939.

The Good, the Bad, and the Ugly. Dir. Sergio Leone. 1966.

The Great Northfield Minnesota Raid. Dir. Philip Kaufman. Robertson and Associates/Universal, 1971.

The Great Train Robbery. Dir. Edwin S. Porter. Edison, 1903.

A Gunfight. Dir. Lamont Johnson. Perf. Johnny Cash and Kirk Douglas. 1970.

The Gunfighter. Dir. Henry King. 1950.

Heaven's Gate. Dir. Michael Cimino. 1980.

High Noon. Dir. Fred Zinnemann. Kramer/UA, 1952.

High Plains Drifter. Dir. Clint Eastwood. 1972.

Into the West. Dir. Robert Dornhelm et al. Alianza, 2005.

I Shot Jesse James. Dir. Samuel Fuller. Lippert, 1948.

Jesse James. Dir. Henry King. 20th Century Fox, 1939.
Johnny Guitar. Dir. Nicholas Ray. Republic, 1953.
The Last Days of Frank and Jesse James. Dir. William A. Graham. 1986.
Last of the Mohicans. Dir. Michael Mann. 1992.
Lightning Jack. Dir. Simon Wincer. 1994.
Little Big Man. Dir. Arthur Penn. Hiller-Stockbridge, 1970.
Lonely Are the Brave. Dir. David Miller. Joel/Universal-International, 1961.
Lonesome Cowboys. Dir. Andy Warhol. Factory, 1968.
The Long Riders. Dir. Walter Hill. 1980.
The Machinist. Dir. Brad Anderson. Filmax, 2004.
The Magnificent Seven. Dir. John Sturges. 1960.
A Man Called Horse. Dir. Elliot Silverstein. Cinema Center, 1970.
Man of the West. Dir. Anthony Mann. 1958.
Maverick. Dir. Richard Donner. 1994.
McCabe & Mrs. Miller. Dir. Robert Altman. Warner, 1970.
The Missing. Dir. Ron Howard. Perf. Tommy Lee Jones, Cate Blanchett, and Eric Schweig. Columbia, 2003.
The Missouri Breaks. Dir. Arthur Penn. 1976.
Monte Walsh. William A. Fraker. Palladian, 1970.
My Darling Clementine. Dir. John Ford. 20th Century Fox, 1946.
No Country For Old Men. Dir. Joel Coen. 2007.
Once Upon a Time in the West. Dir. Sergio Leone. Rafran-San Marco/Paramount, 1968.
Open Range. Dir. Kevin Costner. Perf. Costner, Robert Duvall, and Annette Bening. Touchstone, 2003.
The Outlaw Josey Wales. Dir. Clint Eastwood. 1976.
Pale Rider. Dir. Clint Eastwood. Warner, 1985.
Pat Garret and Billy the Kid. Dir. Sam Peckinpah. Carrol/Fox-MGM, 1973.
The Professionals. Dir. Richard Brooks. 1966.
The Proposition. Dir. John Hillcoat. 2004.
The Quick and the Dead. Dir. Sam Raimi. 1995.
Rambo: First Blood Part Two. Dir. George P. Cosmatos. Kassar/Vajna, 1985.
Ride the High Country. Dir. Sam Peckinpah. MGM, 1961.
Rio Bravo. Dir. Howard Hawks. Perf. John Wayne. Armada/Warner, 1958.
The Searchers. Dir. John Ford. Perf. John Wayne. Warner, 1956.
Seraphim Falls. Dir. David Von Ancken. Icon, 2006.
Silverado. Dir. Lawrence Kasden. 1985.
Shane. Dir. George Stevens. Perf. Van Heflin. Paramount, 1953.
Shanghai Knights. Dir. David Dobkin. All Knight, 2003.
Shanghai Noon. Dir. Tom Dey. Chan, 2000.
Shenandoah. Dir. Andrew V. McLaglen. Universal, 1964.
Smoke Signals. Dir. Chris Eyre. 1998.
Soldier Blue. Dir. Ralph Nelson. Katzka-Berne, 1970.
Stagecoach. Dir. John Ford. Wanger/UA, 1939.

There Will Be Blood. Dir. Paul Thomas Anderson. Ghoulardi, 2007.

The Three Burials of Melquiades Estrada. Dir. Tommy Lee Jones. EuropaCorp, 2005.

3:10 to Yuma. Dir. Delmer Daves. Perf. Van Heflin and Glenn Ford. Columbia, 1956.

3:10 to Yuma. Dir. James Mangold. Perf. Christian Bale and Russell Crowe. Lionsgate, 2007.

Thunderheart. Dir. Michael Apted. 1992.

True Grit. Dir. Henry Hathaway. Perf. John Wayne. Wallis/Paramount, 1969.

The True Story of Jesse James. Dir. Nicholas Ray. 20th Century Fox, 1957.

Ulzana's Raid. Dir. Robert Aldrich. 1972.

Unforgiven. Dir. Clint Eastwood. 1992.

The Virginian. Dir. Victor Fleming. 1929.

Westward the Women. Dir. William A. Wellman. MGM, 1951.

The Wild Bunch. Dir. Sam Peckinpah. Warner, 1969.

Wyatt Earp. Dir. Lawrence Kasdan. Warner, 1994.

Young Guns. Dir. Christopher Cain. Morgan Creek, 1988.

Primary Sources

Alexie, Sherman. *The Lone Ranger and Tonto Fistfight in Heaven*. London: Secker, 1994.

Wister, Owen. *The Virginian*. New York: n.p., 1947.

Hansen, Ron. *The Assassination of Jesse James by the Coward Robert Ford*. London: Grafton, 1983.

Secondary Sources

Arthur, Paul. "How the West Was Spun: *McCabe & Mrs. Miller* and Genre Revisionism." *Cineaste* Summer 2003: 18-20.

Bartley, Paula, and Cathy Loxton. *Plains Women: Women in the American West*. Cambridge: Cambridge UP, 1991.

Bell, James. "Jesse James: Man Behind the Myth." *Sight & Sound* Dec. 2007: 19.

Belton, John. *American Cinema/American Culture*. New York: McGraw-Hill, 1994.

Boddy, William. "'Sixty Million Viewers Can't Be Wrong': The Rise and Fall of the Television Western." *Back in the Saddle Again: New Essays on the Western*. Eds. Edward Buscombe and Roberta E. Pearson. London: BFI, 1998.

Bogue, Allan G. "An Agricultural Empire." *The Oxford History of the American West*. Eds. Clyde A. Milner II, Carol A. O'Connor, and Martha A. Sandweiss. New York: Oxford UP, 1994. 275-313.

Brown, Richard Maxwell. "Violence." *The Oxford History of the American West.* Eds. Clyde A. Milner II, Carol A. O'Connor, and Martha A. Sandweiss. New York: Oxford UP, 1994. 393-425.

Bruckner, Ulrich P. *Für ein paar Leichen mehr: Der Italo-Western von seinen Anfängen bis heute.* Berlin: Schwarzkopf, 2006.

Buscombe, Edward. "Man to Man." *Sight & Sound* Jan 2006: 34-36.

---. Rev. of *All the Pretty Horses*, dir. Billy Bob Thornton. *Sight & Sound* Mar. 2001: 38.

---. Rev. of *Gods and Generals*, dir. Ronald F. Maxwell. *Sight & Sound* Sep. 2003: 50-51.

---. Rev. of *Open Range*, dir. Kevin Costner. *Sight & Sound* Apr. 2004: 62.

---. Rev. of *Seraphim Falls*, dir. David Von Ancken. *Sight & Sound* Sep. 2007: 76.

---. Rev. of *The Alamo*, dir. John Lee Hancock. *Sight & Sound* Sep. 2004: 53-54.

---. Rev. of *The Assassination of Jesse James by the Coward Robert Ford*, dir. Andrew Dominik. *Sight & Sound* Dec. 2007: 51.

---. Rev. of *The Three Burials of Melquiades Estrada*, dir. Tommy Lee Jones. *Sight & Sound* Apr. 2006: 76.

---. "The Homecoming." *Sight & Sound* Feb. 2004: 32-33.

Butler, Anne M. "Selling the Popular Myth." *The Oxford History of the American West.* Eds. Clyde A. Milner II, Carol A. O'Connor, and Martha A. Sandweiss. New York: Oxford UP, 1994. 771-801.

Cameron, Ian, and Douglas Pye, Eds. *The Book of Westerns.* New York: Continuum, 1996.

Cawelti, John G. *The Six-Gun Mystique.* Bowling Green: Bowling Green UP, [1981].

Champagne, Duane, ed. *Chronology of Native American History: From Pre-Columbian Times to the Present.* Detroit: Gale, 1994.

Churchill, Ward. "Fantasies of the Master Race: Categories of Stereotyping of American Indians in Film." *Film and Theory: An Anthology.* Eds. Robert Stam and Toby Miller. Malden: Blackwell, 2000. 697-703.

Clint Eastwood: Ein Cowboy auf dem Weg zum Ruhm. Kabel 1. 29 May 2005.

Denn sie kannten kein Erbarmen: Der Italowestern. ORF 2. 9 Dec. 2007.

Dippie, Brian W. "The Visual West." *The Oxford History of the American West.* Eds. Clyde A. Milner II, Carol A. O'Connor, and Martha A. Sandweiss. New York: Oxford UP, 1994. 675-705.

Drysdale, David. "'Law and Every Other Damn Thing.' Authority, Bad Faith, and the Unlikely Success of Deadwood." *Reading Deadwood: A Western to Swear By.* Ed. David Lavery. London: Tauris, 2006. 133-144.

DTV-Lexikon. 20 vols. München: DTV, 1995.

Evans, Peter William. "*Westward the Women*: Feminising the Wilderness." *The Book of Westerns.* Eds. Ian Cameron and Douglas Pye. New York: Continuum, 1996. 206-213.

Fenin, George N., and William K. Everson. *The Western: From Silents to the Seventies.* Rev. ed. Harmondsworth: Penguin, 1973.

Frayling, Christopher. *Something to Do with Death: Sergio Leone.* London: Faber, 2000.

---. *Spaghetti Westerns: Cowboys and Europeans from Karl May to Sergio Leone.* Rev. ed. London: Tauris, 1998.

Gale, Dennis E. *Understanding Urban Unrest: From Reverend King to Rodney King.* Thousand Oaks: Sage, 1996.

Gilbey, Ryan. Rev. of *Brokeback Mountain*, dir. Ang Lee. *Sight & Sound* Jan. 2006: 50-51.

Grist, Leighton. "Unforgiven." *The Book of Westerns.* Eds. Ian Cameron and Douglas Pye. New York: Continuum, 1996. 294-301.

Grob, Norbert, and Bernd Kiefer. "Heaven's Gate – Das Tor zum Himmel." *Filmgenres: Western.* Eds. Bernd Kiefer and Norbert Grob. Stuttgart: Reclam, 2003. 336-342.

Hanisch, Michael. *Western: Die Entwicklung eines Filmgenres.* Berlin: Henschel, 1984.

Heller, Arno. *Amerikanischer Südwesten: Geschichte, Kultur, Mythos.* Innsbruck: Innsbruck UP, 2006.

---. E-mail to the author. 23 Jan. 2008.

Hembus, Joe. *Das Western-Lexikon: 1567 Filme von 1894 bis heute.* Ed. Benjamin Hembus. München: Heyne, 1995.

---. *Western Geschichte 1540 - 1894: Chronologie, Mythologie, Filmographie.* München: Heyne, 1979.

Howard, Ron. "Ron Howard erzählt von..." *The Missing.* Dir. Ron Howard. DVD. Columbia, 2003.

Jojola, Ted. "Hollywood Goes to the Indians." *Hollywood's Indian: The Portrayal of the Native American in Film.* Eds. Peter C. Rollins and John E. O'Connor. Kentucky: UP of Kentucky, 1998. 12-26.

Kiefer, Bernd. "Erbarmunglos." *Filmgenres: Western.* Eds. Bernd Kiefer and Norbert Grob. Stuttgart: Reclam, 2003. 350-355.

Kilpatrick, Jacquelyn. *Celluloid Indians: Native Americans and Film.* Lincoln: U of Nebraska, 1999.

Kitses, Jim. "Bloodred Horizons." *Sight & Sound* Mar. 2001: 12-15.

---. "Days of the Dead." *Sight & Sound* Apr. 2006: 14-18.

---. "Forgiven." *Sight & Sound* Apr. 2004: 24-27.

---. *Horizons West: Directing the Western from John Ford to Clint Eastwood.* New ed. London: BFI, 2004.

---. "Twilight of the Idol." *Sight & Sound* Dec. 2007: 16-20.

Last, Kevin. "A Quiet American." Letter. *Sight & Sound* Nov. 2007: 96.

---. "Western Values." Letter. *Sight & Sound* May 2004: 88.

Lavery, David, ed. *Reading Deadwood: A Western to Swear By.* London: Tauris, 2006.

Lenihan, John H. *Showdown: Confronting Modern America in the Western Film*. Urbana: U of Illinois, 1980.

Leonardy, Heribert J. *Der Mythos vom "edlen" Räuber: Untersuchungen narrativer Tendenzen und Bearbeitungsformen bei den vier Räuberfiguren Robin Hood, Schinderhannes, Jesse James und Ned Kelly*. Saarbrücken: Schneidewind, 1997.

Macnab, Geoffrey. Rev. of *3:10 to Yuma*, dir. James Mangold. *Sight & Sound* Nov. 2007: 80.

McCrisken, Trevor B., and Andrew Pepper. *American History and Contemporary Hollywood Film*. Edinburgh: Edinburgh UP, 2005.

Milner, Clyde A., II, Carol A. O'Connor, and Martha A. Sandweiss, eds. *The Oxford History of the American West*. New York: Oxford UP, 1994.

Milner, Clyde A., II, Anne M. Butler, and David Rich Lewis, eds. *Major Problems in the History of the American West: Documents and Essays*. 2nd ed. Major Problems in American History Ser. Boston: Houghton, 1997.0,30cm

Moses, Dirk A., ed. *Genocide and Settler Society: Frontier Violence and Stolen Indigenous Children in Australian History*. New York: Berghahn, 2004.

O'Connor, John E. "The White Man's Indian: An Institutional Approach." *Hollywood's Indian: The Portrayal of the Native American in Film*. Eds. Peter C. Rollins and John E. O'Connor. Kentucky: UP of Kentucky, 1998. 27-38.

O'Hehir, Andrew. "Way Down West." *Sight & Sound* June 2004: 6.

Parkinson, Michael, and Clyde Jeavons. *A Pictorial History of Westerns*. Rev. ed. London: Hamlyn, 1983.

Rauscher, Andreas. "Silverado." *Filmgenres: Western*. Eds. Bernd Kiefer and Norbert Grob. Stuttgart: Reclam, 2003. 342-345.

Roddick, Nick. "Ballad of the Wild Boys." *Sight & Sound* Mar. 2006: 26-29.

Rollins, Peter C., and John E. O'Connor, eds. *Hollywood's Indian: The Portrayal of the Native American in Film*. Kentucky: UP of Kentucky, 1998.

"Sam Peckinpah's West: Das Vermächtnis eines Hollywood-Abtrünnigen." *The Wild Bunch*. Dir. Sam Peckinpah. 1969. DVD. Warner, 2006.

Saunders, John. *The Western Genre: From Lordsburg to Big Whiskey*. Short Cuts Ser. London: Wallflower, 2001.

Seeßlen, Georg, and Claudius Weil. *Western-Kino: Geschichte und Mythologie des Western-Films*. Grundlagen des populären Films 1. Reinbek: Rowohlt, 1979.

Sharrett, Christopher. Rev. of *Gods and Generals*, dir. Ronald Maxwell. *Cineaste* Summer 2003: 36-38.

Shivley, JoEllen. "Cowboys and Indians: Perceptions of Western Films Among American Indians and Anglos." *Film and Theory: An Anthology*. Eds. Robert Stam and Toby Miller. Malden: Blackwell, 2000. 345-360.

Skelsey, Philip. Letter. *Sight & Sound* Nov. 2007: 96.
Smith, Grahame. Letter. *Sight & Sound* Sep. 2006: 96.
Smith, Paul. *Clint Eastwood: A Cultural Production*. American Culture 8. Minneapolis: U of Minneasota, 1993.
Snodgrass, Mary Ellen. *Encyclopedia of Frontier Literature*. New York: Oxford UP, 1997.
Spencer, Liese. Rev. of *The Proposition*, dir. John Hillcoat. *Sight & Sound* Mar. 2006: 72.
Spiel mir das Lied vom Western. Dir. Alain Lasfa0,30cmrgues. Arte. 10 Sep. 1995.
Szalosky, Melinda. "A Tale N/nobody Can Tell: The Return of a Repressed Western History in Jim Jarmusch's *Dead Man*." *Westerns: Films Through History*. Ed. Janet Walker. AFI Film Readers Ser. New York: Routledge, 2001. 47-69.
Tavernier, Bertrand. "The Ethical Romantic." *Film Comment* Jan.-Feb. 2003: 42-49.
Thomson, David. "The Last Frontier." *Sight & Sound* Feb. 2004: 12-15.
Tompkins, Jane. *West of Everything: The Inner Life of Westerns*. New York: Oxford UP, 1992.
Tuska, Jon. *The American West in Film: Critical Approaches to the Western*. Westport: Greenwood, 1985.

Uebbing, Sandra. *Amerika (er-)finden: Tradition und Transformation von Mythen in Filmen von Sergio Leone*. München: Fischer, 2007.
Walker, Michael. "The Westerns of Delmer Daves." *The Book of Westerns*. Eds. Ian Cameron and Douglas Pye. New York: Continuum, 1996. 123-160.
Walters, Ben. Rev. of *The Missing*, dir. Ron Howard. *Sight & Sound* Mar. 2004: 50.
Weidinger, Martin. *Nationale Mythen - männliche Helden: Politik und Geschlecht im amerikanischen Western*. Frankfurt: Campus, 2006.
---. "Re: Nationale Mythen - männliche Helden und aktuelle Western." E-mail to the author. 31 Mar. 2008.
White, Richard. "Outlaw Gangs and Social Bandits." *Major Problems in the History of the American West. Documents and Essays*. Eds. Clyde A Milner II, Anne M. Butler, and David Rich Lewis. 2nd ed. Major Problems in American History Ser. Boston: Houghton, 1997. 222-237.
Wright, Will. *Sixguns and Society: A Structural Study of the Western*. Berkeley: U of California, 1975.

Index

Zeittracht Medien GmbH
Ferdinand-Jühlke-Straße 7
99095 Erfurt, Deutschland
produktsicherheit@kolibri360.de